# I TRIED TO RUN
# A RAILWAY

## GERARD FIENNES

WITH A FOREWORD BY CHRISTIAN
WOLMAR AND NICHOLAS FAITH

HEAD
ZEUS

*An Apollo Book*

First published by Ian Allan Ltd in 1967

Revised edition published in the UK in 2016 by Head of Zeus Ltd
This Apollo paperback edition published in 2018 by Head of Zeus Ltd

1 3 5 7 9 10 8 6 4 2

A catalogue record for this book is available from the British Library.

ISBN (PB) 9781786691286
ISBN (E) 9781784970840

Printed and bound by CPI Group (UK) Ltd, Croydon, CR0 4YY

# CONTENTS

# FOREWORD

Quirky, whimsical, eccentric, iconoclastic, funny and at times, completely incomprehensible, this is the book that railway managers always refer to when asked to choose one that explains how a railway operates and how best to manage it.

*I Tried to Run a Railway* is unique in its hilarity; there are not many others in Wolmar's Railway Library that can lay claim to laugh-out-loud moments. Nor are there many accounts of a business career that are so honest about the protagonist's own failings. Fiennes' self-deprecating humour is in evidence right from the start; he laughs off his own mistakes, which allows him to be a harsh critic of his colleagues and he is also very honest about how he learns from them.

Fiennes' account of the operation of Britain's railways from the 1930s to the 1960s describes a world that no longer exists. It is a world of coal and dirt; steel and noise; smoke and cloth-capped men that is so alien and so different that it seems as remote as classical history.

Both pre- and post-nationalisation, the railway employed huge numbers of staff with multiple layers of management. It ran a vast array of services, from slow passenger trains and expresses to coal and general freight trains that required extensive marshalling yards where the clunk of wagons being shunted and gently connected seemed to ring out endlessly.

British Rail at its creation in 1948 employed more than 600,000 people. Their job descriptions, too, such as Traffic Apprentice and Chief Signalling Inspector have long disappeared. So has the practice of sending staff around the country to do jobs that could vary from running a goods depot to being a stationmaster. Today, railway managers barely understand different parts of the railway in which they have never had any direct involvement.

It was a time when derailments were commonplace and accidents an accepted part of the industry, so railway managers like Fiennes were expected to sort out both major and minor mishaps. He describes with great feeling a disaster at Gidea Park and the efforts that went into restoring service quickly – something that does not happen today. The efforts to discover precisely what happened were meticulous too, and he is not above accusing several of those involved of having lied.

While the railway has a completely different structure today and the technology has been transformed, do not make the mistake that it was only when the railways were privatised that concerns about cutting costs or gaining new business first came to the fore. Fiennes was always on the look out for better ways of doing things, even if sometimes his solutions were not the right ones. He understood the commercial imperatives of getting as many passengers as possible using the railway. Moreover, he was clear about the limitations of his responsibility, stressing that it was the politicians who had to make decisions over unprofitable lines.

Fiennes rose – bumpily – to chief operating officer of British Railways and it was only then that he was really able to apply new thinking to an old industry, introducing new processes and even querying whether there was at all a need for marshalling yards while vast ones were still being planned and built. They were, of course, soon all closed a couple of decades after his departure, having sucked up huge amounts of investment expenditure that Fiennes had warned against.

This book has a wider resonance than the railways. It is about coping with the pressures of working in a big organisation and the way that decisions – good and bad – are made. That is why it remains as Roger Ford of *Modern Railways* put it "a train operators guide for the 21st century". In particular, Fiennes rails against the constant reorganisations that dogged his career.

Fiennes, too, deserves a special accolade because the book resulted in his sacking. The bosses at British Railways were not amused by his criticism of constant reorganisations and of the incompetence of some of his colleagues, and showed him the door. However, Fiennes had the last laugh. He went on to be a director of Ian Allan, the company that originally published his book.

Christian Wolmar and Nicholas Faith 2015

# INTRODUCTION

I came down from Oxford in 1928 to make my way in the world. I had no vocation and no money. I had a fourth class degree in Greats which was a charitable way of the examiners saying: 'We would fail you if we did our duty'; a job with the L.N.E.R. and acute claustrophobia in trains.

The job with the L.N.E.R. and its heirs is what this story is about. There is little about high policy. Nor is it about the future of railways. Plenty of others can tell us about that—at any given time: different times, different futures. The only certainty, past and present, is that each Railway or Transport Act ensures the next. The story is about someone who came slowly and reluctantly to grips with the basic realities of a railway job and against all expectations and reason was absorbed by the magic of the thing.

The job happened to me quite unexpectedly. My father had died in my first year up at Oxford. Mother had four younger sons and little money. I had borrowed over £300 from the College. Jobs in 1928 were hard to come by. I said 'snap' to the first employer who offered me one.

*

So ran the introduction to the original hardback book published in 1967. In 1973, this chapter was revised to relate some of the events of 1967 which culminated in my abrupt departure from British Railways by summary invitation. About that departure let me say that I have known for long enough that my most logical management decisions turn about and look at me upside down. Such is the essence of farce. Therefore at that time and in that matter neither the publishers of the book nor the British Railways Board who unanimously invited my departure were responsible for their actions. I was.

Gerard Fiennes

# ILLUSTRATIONS

# 1

## THE WAY IN

The L.N.E.R's system for training Traffic Apprentices was run pretty well single-handed by the Assistant General Manager, Robert Bell. He selected a few men from the salaried staff, ostensibly by competitive examination; handpicked a few more direct from the minor public and grammar schools; and got the remainder via the Appointments Boards at the Universities.

He had principles. One of them was no nepotism. Few sons, nephews or cousins of the Directors came on to the L.N.E.R. If one did, his life was especially difficult. I can't remember one even lasting the course, let alone rising in the service. Secondly, the L.N.E.R. was poor but honest. Traffic Apprentices were the same. He said to me in his slow, dry Scots, 'You may expect, if you are successful, to become a District Officer at a salary of £800 a year'. Ten years later he appointed E. J. Stephens to District Superintendent, Lincoln, at £700. We were certainly poorer. Thirdly, there was to be no skulking around within reach of home. Scotsmen and Geordies went to the Southern Area; Cockneys went to Scotland. Luckily mother was in Brittany and I drew the south. Fourthly, there must be no communication. Two Traffic

Apprentices together is no Traffic Apprentice. Lastly the basic railway is what matters. Training was at stations, small and large, marshalling yards, locomotive depots, control offices, offices for timing and diagramming, and for townsmen and claims.

We spoke to an officer perhaps ten times a year. We were taught our trade by the men who plied those trades. At the time I missed the point. I went slavishly on training as if it was a projection of school. I hadn't a clue of the pattern and purpose behind it all. I was, as Dillington House has so rightly said of Traffic Apprentices like me—'a thrombosis: a bloody clot in the system'.

This lack of direction soon caught up with me. After six months I had an accident on a motor cycle—Brother Dick's in fact—and spent a year in hospital, not getting over the accident, which was of little consequence, but letting Psychiatrist Mark Palmer sort out the mental tangles. I remember he talked very largely about sex.

Mark didn't cure the claustrophobia in trains. He did nevertheless put a bit of fight into me. I wrote earlier 'the job "happened" to me quite unexpectedly'. Events were always taking me by surprise. Becoming senior prefect of a house, getting colours, an exhibition, captain of cricket at Hertford. I hadn't worked for any of these things. Mark did a lot for my intentions. And the first intention was to get over the claustrophobia. So with the sweat rolling off me I rode from Tunbridge Wells Central to West; then next day to Tonbridge and so on. Mark seemed to be right. I didn't throw myself out, or faint, or die. It was hell.

I came on the next good thing very quickly. 'R.B.' (Bell) sent me to Hatfield on the Great Northern main line. I walked into the Station Master's office and into R. B. (Dick) Temple. He was in his shirt sleeves. He had covered his desk with small slips of paper. 'Come and help me sort this out' was his greeting. He was doing the Guards' workings for the St. Alban's, Luton, Welwyn, Hitchin

and Baldock services. It was not his job but District Office's. This
love of other people's jobs was his outstanding habit.

We went on playing this variation of scrabble for some time.
At the end he had saved two guards and a lot of overtime. He
thought District Office would not be pleased. As the years went
by I came to see the advantage, indeed the necessity, of having a
Dick Temple or a Philip Shirley in the organisation; but not more
than one. For my part I have always found more than enough
to do in the job which my masters have set me and repeatedly
refuse to swan around outside it. Contrariwise I resent and resist
irrelevant people butting into mine. Nevertheless, when Philip
Shirley (then financial member of the British Railways Board)
rings up on a hot Sunday and says 'Gerry, I am sitting in a garden
at Retford. A train has just gone up with a Pacific engine, a brake
van and 14 wagons' I take notice. This train does not run on the
next or any subsequent Sunday. This principle of getting a 'prod'
of this sort into the outfit to keep it on the hop has held good for
me since I became District Superintendent at Stratford: Stuart
Ward, Douglas Fenton, Sidney Millard and Freddie Wright have
been often great and enduring nuisances and distractions, but of
great and enduring value.

To this principle I add one proviso—that the 'prod' does
his proper job as well as other people's. In later life Dick Temple
forgot this. He became the Traffic Manager at Sheffield in 1957
when I became Line Traffic Manager at King's Cross. And the punctuality of the passenger service went to rags and ruin. Stuart Ward,
the Operating Superintendent under me, decided that I would have
to take this thing out of the Traffic Managers' hands and restore
the pure operating responsibility from Superintendent to District
Superintendent. Now Dick was a very Senior Statesman. So
when, at the meeting of Traffic Managers about this, he froze
and said 'Does this mean that you have no confidence in your

Traffic Managers to run trains to time? It took more courage than I knew I had to look him in the eye and reply 'Yes, Dick; that is just what I do mean'. In two months Stuart Ward and Sidney Millard had us at the top of the league.

At the moment in 1930 though, Dick and I are not eyeball to eyeball. He is in six months going to report whether I am competent to issue tickets, do the daily balance, passenger classification, monthly balance and returns, passenger and freight; whether I can get 80 trusses of hay into a wagon, sheet and rope it correctly, use a shunting pole and brake stick. I am pretty sure he never encouraged me to roll two milk churns at a time. I rolled one of the two down the ramp under an express. The air was full of whining metal; and later of whining rockets from District Office. He took my part with them, bless him; but at the end I didn't match the standard which he set for himself.

In the next two and a half years the programme took me to London, Manchester, Leeds, Southend and Parkeston. I went on learning by rote and not by understanding. Nevertheless by this method examinations came easily to me. The last and crowning glory was the oral examination in Rules & Regulations in front of the Superintendent's Chief Signalling Inspector, Rickett. He grilled me for three hours. I was, I believe, word perfect, because I had learned by heart the Block Regulations for double and single lines, the Guard's Rules and the Rules of Single Line Working. Mind you, I had a great grandfather who, when at the end of one term of Winchester, was asked what he offered for repetition, replied 'The Iliad and the Odyssey of Homer; the Aeneid and the Eclogues of Virgil'. He could learn a thousand lines before breakfast; and maybe some of the genes came through the generations. I found out how little actual understanding I had when a year later I found myself putting in single line working in emergency between Whitemoor Junction and Coldham. But as always at Whitemoor there was somebody to tell the incompetent how to do it: in this case, the signalman on duty, Bob Wright.

There were not many highlights of that time; some days relaying in the torrent of air which sweeps through Woodhead tunnel, grim moments on the footplates of up trains slipping in the tunnel in a smother of smoke and steam with the fireman and myself down on hands and knees in search of breath for long past eternity; building a brick arch in a Claud which stood up for weeks; doing tubes in the fireboxes of Clauds at night between the evening and morning diagrams with anything up to 30 lbs. of steam in the boiler. Of these 8821 had an oval firebox door which led to me getting in and expanding not only the tubes so that they were watertight, but myself so that I was too tight a fit to emerge. Charlie Hobbs and Maurice his mate, stood on the footplate outside giving advice between gusts of Homeric laughter. That I should take all my clothes off was common ground. Where they were divided was whether they should pull me out over the sizzling firehole door face upwards and scald my bottom or face downwards with effects on posterity unborn. In the event I took my meals off the mantelpiece for a few days.

One of the lessons which I learned was to estimate accurately an opponent's reach. One night I crossed the bridge at Nottingham Victoria to see a scene of great activity below. Nottingham Forest had been playing Hull. The Hooligans were on their way home. In some it had gone to their legs; they were playing ring-a-ring-o'roses on the platform. In some it had gone to their heads. They were wandering off into Weekday Cross tunnel and laying their fevered brows on the nice cool rails. Many, urged by who knows what dim motivation, were getting into compartments, lurching straight through and clambering on to the track on the offside. It was all movement and far beyond the abilities of the station staff. However we rounded up a few volunteers to do a mopping up operation on the permanent way; we stationed a few with carriage cleaning brushes on the offside of the train to lock what doors they could and to poke in the snoot any head which appeared; and the rest of us grabbed the reeling mob on the platform one by one and bundled them into the train. My last task was a little old woman in black; she was hopping around like a gym instructress with a resolute and austere look on her face; probably she had lost her Salvation Army hat; she was wielding a handbag like a flail. I ducked under the bag, grabbed her round the middle, bundled her in, slammed the door, and stood for a moment triumphant.

Down came the window, out shot a telescopic left, and I had the shiner of all time for weeks.

The two months at Parkeston were also a highlight, not by reason of the work, which was agreeable, but irrelevant, because even poor men could not get through the eye of the needle into the Heaven of the Continental Department, but because Norrie was there. And it was spring and the easterlies turned us into roaring lions. We tamed our appetites with golf and tennis and hockey and football and courting and dancing. I can't remember ever having gone or wanting to go to bed. When I later got on to the training committee I took care to withdraw Parkeston from the schedule of training. Two years afterwards when we could afford it Norrie and I married.

In the meantime I had my training shortened by six months and went off to York as a temporary wagon inspector for the winter. This was fun for three reasons. The first was that we hunted in couples and the other half of mine was Jimmie Lisle. We toured the Southern Area of the L.N.E.R. denouncing during the day with the utmost ferocity the misuse of wagons, but in the evening turning up at the local badminton club and challenging their champions for beer. The second was that for the first time I flexed an executive muscle. Away from Jimmie for some reason on one frosty morning

THE WAY IN 11

I went round Boston Dock and found 100 'highs' more than the agent had declared on his stock report. Before I left I had seen two trains on their way to Hull. I was at last some value in the world. The third was that I found that the use of Butter Vans at Parkeston Quay left a lot to be desired, whereas Norrie's company and help in tracing them were wholly desirable. I was sorry when after five months I was appointed Assistant Yard Master at Whitemoor.

# PAIGNTON

## GLORIOUS SOUTH DEVON

Guide from Dept. P. Entertainments Manager. Paignton

# 2

## YARDS AND CONTROL

Whoever made the plan did better for me than he knew. I am sure he never meant it as more than an economy but he made an inspector redundant and laid it upon the two A.Y.M.'s, ex-Goods Guard Bill Dring and myself to work every second week the 6 a.m. Inspector's turn in the Down Yard.

I could no longer be a learner. I had to be a Doer. If there was no signalman in Grassmoor Junction to let the engine with the meat from the London Docks off the 1.35 a.m. Temple Mills across from the Down side to the Up to connect with the 7.10 a.m. to Wisbech and King's Lynn, there was nobody to open, work and close the box but me. When I came on duty the night Inspector, Jim Page, tall, whitehaired, red cheeked and light blue of eye, would hold out a fistful of telegrams. 'Harrer, Harrer, Harrer'. The code word for 'wire forward' was 'Arrow'. 'Look at this lot', he would say, 'find them, boy'. Hence my ingrained habit of looking at wagon labels. One which I never found was a van of passengers' luggage in advance for Scarborough in the height of the holiday season. Five days after it was missed the L.N.E.R. offered a reward of £5 for its recovery. The prize was won by

Class 3 Shunter, Harold West, who we calculated later must have himself shunted it into the siding for empty vans.

For a while the head shunters, Tommy Woodbine, big George Dobson, Tanky Giddings, carried me as a supercargo. Gradually I began to have the three principles of railway work; a sense of order, a sense of time, and a sense of money. Bill Dring and I got to know how to work the console of points and the retarders in the Up and Down Yards. At the beginning it was often an hour's work to square up the Jam that Mother made. I learned how to re-rail wagons and engines without sending for the crane and how to square the ganger into replacing the few chairs without making a report. I released one day the engine of the 1.35 a.m. Temple Mills and made two mistakes; the first not to notice that the leading wagon was a steam-heater-fitted banana van. The second to report myself for pulling off the steam-heater pipe, when wagon-examiner Rocher Richmond would have replaced it and nothing said.

However much the two mechanised yards were out in front for design, my favourite time was in the evening in Norwood Yard. Norwood has two receptions (the Dirt Track) and 14 sidings. There was a little knuckle off which the vans and highfits and highs used to roll, cut after cut, the wheels ringing high and softly, travelling gently and evenly into their appointed road. We spent little time on closing down or correcting wrong shunts. Percy Baynes, always one handed with the shunting pole looking like a toothpick in his fist, and Hodge Jackman in the ground frame and one chaser would shunt 250 wagons an hour from 5.15 to 7.15. Then the pilot would drop on to No. 8 to push 20 more wagons into the tranship shed. The K.3s of the 7.25 to Liverpool and the 7.30 to Manchester Ducie Street would clank from the engine spur on to their trains; and the fruit and vegetables and potatoes and cider and mustard and imports of East Anglia would stream down the joint line direct to Newcastle and York and the West Riding and Sheffield and Manchester and Liverpool and Nottingham.

Whitemoor was a home of basic English. 'Now' cried Guard Slogger Godfrey, to a Doncaster Driver once when former A.Y.M. Bill Johnson had asked Slogger to get his bloody train out of the yard, 'Now, yer —— long North Country bastard ...' Now and again the biter was bit. I went back along the Down reception lines one morning after a driver had stopped his train roughly, to see whether he had hurt the guard. In the brake, standing holding the wheel was Fred Charles, mouthing fast but inarticulately. He had broken his false teeth. Nor was it all on the staff side. In later years Guard Happy Laws reported A.Y.M. George Gibb, now Chairman of the B.R.S. Federation, to me because he, Happy, himself no slouch at basic English, was revolted by George's language.

Cricket was with March Town. I still use on ceremonial occasions the bat which they gave me when I got 100 not out in 35 minutes against Wimblington and had to console their fairly fast bowler, Arthur Peacock, by getting him tight. Cricket also with a shunters' side which Driver Davis, now Mayor of Southend, Guard Jimmy Lord, Shunter Charlie Northfield and I started in a field among the cow pats. Football was with Dan Orbell and with (for obvious reasons) Hock'em Bougen from which I carry the scars to this day. After one game Dan's wife turned up at the local, 'Come home, Dan. You may be foreman down Whitemoor but not when I'm here'. Then Norrie and I married and moved into a tiny house with no garden in Regent Avenue, March. The Yard gave us a lot of china, so indestructible that we still have it, and used to leave anonymous cauliflowers and potatoes and carrots on the doorstep. Once there was a hare. Norrie said she would try to cook it, if I would skin it. I set to. At the end of a couple of hours, bloody, bold and resolute, I searched the remains. We never did find the fourth leg.

Norrie led naturally to a lot less beer and cricket. We put tennis in its place and toured the county pot hunting. We weren't a lot of good at this because although Norrie was way out of my class, I was enthusiastic and used to poach. She used to get wild with me and then to fall into helpless laughter with the result that before we pulled ourselves together the match was gone. The crown of these experiences was at Haddenham. Remember that we were very poor. We started life with me having just paid off my Oxford debt and having nothing. Norrie had £350, out of which we had spent £100 on furnishing two bedrooms and one sitting room. Therefore, when we looked at the prizes at Haddenham and Norrie said aloud 'What we have come for is a dining room carpet' she more than half meant it. We got into the final before a large and hostile crowd. At every burst of barracking, remembering this dining room carpet, we fell into more and more helpless laughter. This in the face of anger is still a habit of mine. On the day before writing this page, Pearson Armstrong, A.G.M. (Staff) at York, came into my room as pleased as punch because Bill Buxton, his Industrial Relations Officer, had negotiated a settlement with the Unions about conductor guards on the rural railways in East Anglia. Bill had achieved a saving of £84,000 a year at a cost of conceding six extra posts, £4,800.

'Why six and not one or 12', I said.

'Oh, well', Pearson at his most Scottish and most deliberate, 'that is just staff negotiation'.

'Haven't staff people heard of work study? How much a conductor guard can do depends on the number of passengers, the time between stops and the system of fares. Does Bill understand this?'

Pearson expecting unstinted praise for Bill because this negotiation had been dragging its feet and having got instead a loaded question was bloody wild.

'Let me tell you, General Manager,...' When he calls me 'General Manager' the claymore is half way out of its sheath. And I fell into helpless and hysterical laughter. He went on looking like Flodden Field for a few moments and then, bless him, fell into laughter himself.

Anyway we lost the match at Haddenham and three moves and four years later, because the L.N.E.R. paid no expenses for removal, we had not £250 but £235 and still no dining room carpet.

Our first move was to Cambridge as Chief Controller. H. F. Sanderson had recently come from Stratford as District Superintendent causing a chain reaction which took Bill Johnson and then Harry Pallant from Cambridge, the first as Chief Freight Trains Clerk to H. H. Mauldin, the second as Assistant Station Master, Liverpool Street. To Sandy, because he was new, I was an unknown quantity. I was also an unknown quantity to the Assistant District Superintendent Bertie Wright whose approach to Whitemoor had so terrified me that I always lit out for the farthest confines of the yard, namely the signal box at Twenty Feet.

I went to Cambridge therefore on probation. However, Norrie and Mabel Sanderson became fast friends and secured my unpromising future. Cambridge was a lovely district. We had a basic heavy trunk haul of coal and goods from Whitemoor direct in train loads to the principal towns of East Anglia. We had a complex network of pick up goods trains. We had a series of seasonal traffics rising and falling rapidly to and from peaks; flowers from Wisbech and the St. Ives loop, strawberries, early plums, late plums, apples, potatoes, sugar beet all in succession from April to February. Except in February and March we had never a dull moment. We had a modest express passenger service with London, both Liverpool Street and King's Cross, and with Liverpool, Newcastle and Birmingham. We had a frequent local service on the main lines and branches. We had horse specials from Newmarket pretty well every day. In the summer we had a great through holiday traffic to Yarmouth and Lowestoft and Clacton.

The Cambridge line was full of trains. In the evening there was no path for a coal train out of Whitemoor for Temple Mills between 6.55 p.m. and midnight. I used to sit now and again in Audley End or Elsenham boxes and watch the stream of express goods pounding up the bank. One after another they came, J39s, J20s, J17s, with lines of dark vans and sheeted highs shouldering and chattering behind them. Before the tail light of one reeled out of sight to the south, the strong beat of the next rose out of the woods to my right. We brooded over those fast goods like hawks. One month, it was certainly May and I think 1936, our express freight punctuality was better than the express passenger. I have never capped that one since.

There was one little bit of planning which was a straw in the wind for me. Years later it became almost a rush of blood to the head about utilisation of locomotives. It started with Sandy urging me to increase the freight train load. Frank Stowe, the Freight Trains Clerk and I, settled down one day with a bunch of journals for coal trains between Whitemoor and Temple Mills. We didn't know what we were looking for. Frank began to grind his teeth. He had a very slow, very thick voice.

'Look', he said, 'another ruddy J15 on this one'.

This was a six coupled long chimney unsuperheated relic which hauled less than half the load of our Class 8 3-cylinder Gresley 02's.

'Well, let's see what the 02's were doing that day'.

Only nine out of our 16 had worked a train 83 miles out and 83 miles home that day. Frank and I settled down to do rough diagrams based on 14 of the 16 02's being in service every day and doing one and a half round trips, 250 miles a day. This in those days was quite something with coal trains. Since Temple Mills was in the Stratford district and therefore the diagrams were inter-district we sent our work up to Bill Johnson. He added the idea of putting a target number on each diagram, which was marked on the card in control and was carried on the buffer beam of the locomotive. The freight train load and the net ton miles per train engine hour in the Cambridge district went up by 20 per cent.

After 18 months, in 1935, I went for an interview with Jenkin-Jones, Superintendent of the North Eastern, for a job as second clerk in the Freight Trains Office headed by George Smith who had been for part of the time my boss at Whitemoor. Half way through the interview, which seemed to be going all right, J.J. said 'I suppose you can do advanced mathematics?'

I sat disconsolate for a moment then rose to my feet and said 'No sir. Not a hope'.

I went to the door, bethought myself and asked 'What do you mean by advanced mathematics, sir?'

'Simple equations ...' I retraced my steps, sat down and got the job. This was lucky because now mathematics is even less advanced by reason of having to translate it all into binary for the benefit of that dunce, the computer.

York had many advantages. The first was the head of the Freight Section George Smith. He had been for part of my time there Yardmaster at Whitemoor. So it was a bit of an uplift that he didn't veto a second spell of my company. He was a good organisation man and kept the job in fair order. He was one of those little men with a face like a puzzled pug, at which it always made me cheerful to look. The Hun had shot him in the bottom in the war so that he strode around pigeon-toed with his left buttock convoluting in a corkscrew roll. This was even after years a never failing source of fun.

George was driving along a programme of accelerating freight trains by fully or partly fitting them with the vacuum brake.

Since the timings were done by the six District Superintendents life consisted of a series of timing meetings. The diplomacy and patience needed led us to frame proposals for centralising the timing and diagramming at York. At these meetings, Freddie Margetts, now operating member of the B.R.B. who as head of the Freight Train Bonus Section attended now and again, used to sit glaring at one of the District Trains Clerks and muttering under his breath 'The wooden bougger, the wooden bougger'. The other end of the organisation, Fred Nottingham, whose job it was to translate it all into timetables used to take himself off to the printers at Leeds for weeks at a time, slowly and reluctantly and fairly perseveringly getting Rowntree's chocolate from York to London and Cadbury's from Bournville to Newcastle, and the cattle for Foss Islands to start later and arrive earlier.

I was riding last February with Driver Calvert of York who in his firing days was on the Main Line express freight. With his tales of bringing up the Aberdeen Meat, often double-headed with two C.7s, flaring through the night, pretty well regardless of weather, block and block with the sleeping car trains he brought back a vivid memory of sitting with the guard on the verandah step of a brake van of one of these trains approaching Darlington at around 80 m.p.h. holding on like grim death and trusting that exactly that fate would not overtake us at the junction to the station. On the front the C.7s were a good ride, as were the North Eastern B.16s or the occasional Gresley Pacific but can there ever have been an engine as rough at 80 m.p.h. as a Gresley K.3? Nevertheless the Front End ran them. Somehow it had got around that the company had guaranteed an arrival in Smithfield Market by 3 a.m. Calvert reminded me that this was so. And the Front End were going to see, regardless, that the meat was there.

I carried some of that meat when I did a fortnight's training at Farringdon Street in 1930. There is only one way to hump beef weighing over 2 cwt. Lean forward as they dump it on your back and let the momentum keep you going. Your legs daren't give way. Then back for another and another till you are sweating like a bull and weaving on legs that have turned to jelly. The pubs are open and a pint hisses down and steadies you. Go back for a few more sides of beef, then back to the pub. In the few nights I was on that job I must have drunk 11 or 12 pints a night without them having the slightest effect either afterwards or at the time.

While the Freight Trains Section under George Smith and the Passenger under Philip Burtt and the Bonus under Fred Margetts were a relaxed, cheerful and competent lot, in spite of Fred's habit often enough of getting out the press gang to work all night on a scheme, the higher echelons were in the giant class. J.J. himself, Burgoyne and Paul Gibb were a trio of Chief Officers so strong that the clerical staff hardly knew the name of the General Manager. Myself, I used to go on tiptoe past Paul Gibb's room quaking at the roars of rage barely muffled by the door.

Nevertheless one day Phyllis 'Gargie' Gibb turned up at our house and took Norrie off to Brandsby for the afternoon. Thereafter we went over frequently. 'P.G.' taught me to fish for trout and, later in the year, grayling in the Swale. He did a lot of damage to my Bridge by paralysing me with fear. Norrie stood up to him, but then she was pregnant and had a cub to defend. Nowadays in his 80th year, we play with him a lot; family against family. Dummy's hand goes down on the table with a look of pure terror on her face. 'Woman!!' he roars 'How often have I told you that you must (or must not)...'

Jeremy was born in the Purey Cust Nursing Home on March 9th, 1937. There was deep snow which lasted well into the Spring. When Norrie came home our little house in Acomb was cold and damp. We were under orders from Doctor Reggie Lister to see that we maintained strict discipline about feeds. For weeks from 2 a.m.

to 6 a.m. we lay in bed clutching each other, tense and despairing while Gibb-like roars came from next door. From 5.30 p.m. to 5.59 p.m. it was my job to pacify him by carrying him round. Never have I been so tired. Never again did we not feed a baby the moment it indicated a preference.

We played a lot of tennis and a lot of squash, which was the only game at which I was Norrie's master. We were sorry when the summons came to go to Liverpool Street. We packed the beer empties in the pram. We took them to the off-licence and set off to live at Brentwood.

Now in 1937 I was for the first time in contact with H. H. Mauldin, the ex-booking clerk at Ponders End who, through a successful army career in the first war allied to an enormous talent for managing men, had become Superintendent of the Great Eastern. He was known as 'The Colonel' 'The Old Man' 'The Old Bugger' according to mood. I had been in his company before, usually at long range, at the Whitemoor Guards or Ely All Grades Dinner or such. If the Old Man came to a dinner, there was a full house to hear him speak. Relaxed, tall, burly; delight at captivating men beaming on his face—telling tale after tale, usually revolting; never a sermon, seldom anything about railway work, but always about railwaymen. He was to all eyes glad to be among them; proud of the way they worked the Great Eastern; content that they should.

One day he was visiting signalboxes around Bury St. Edmunds. He had been to Cockfield and went on in his car to Welnetham. As he walked up the steps he heard one ring on the block bell. This, for some, is an irregular means of calling your neighbour to the telephone when you don't want the whole circuit to listen. At that moment he remembered he had left his gloves at Cockfield and wanted to tell the signalman to send them on the next train.

'I'll take it' he said and lifted the phone.

Cockfield's voice 'Ey-oop, Joe: the Old Bugger's coming.'

'It's the Old Bugger speaking' said the Old Man with relish.

He was a ready man: an important man but never a self-important man; therefore an easy man. It is part of his magic that people who worked under him came in time to have something of his quality—Harry Pallant, H. C. Johnson, W. G. Thorpe.

Nevertheless he Managed; with a capital M. I first met it at golf. He won his games. Here is a small white ball stationary: no-one will prevent me from hitting it except myself. I know how, so ... cheerful, relaxed, concentrated, short, straight, inexorable. That is why after G. F. Thurston retired, he and the Great Eastern won the race against Barrington-Ward for the vacant General Managership of the Southern Area. I was in his room when B.-W. came to congratulate him, 'So you're the lucky bugger' he began. I was out of earshot for the rest.

Barrington-Ward, now Sir Michael, was then Superintendent of the larger Western Section of the L.N.E.R.'s Southern Area. He had come from the Midland where, as he never tired of telling us, Paget was a hero of Homeric proportions, via the Kaiser's War when he enjoyed putting out fires in ammunition dumps (Lt. Col., D.S.O.) and the North Eastern to the Southern Area.

The Old Man sent for me one day. 'Fiennes' he said; he never used my christian name, 'These Net Ton Miles per train engine hour are shocking'. So they were. He went on to talk apparently at large about what he saw when he was out. I recognised the indirect leads; 'you must get them better soon'. And didn't forget to notice it when they were. Contrariwise last year I was being flayed by a very Exalted Person in a comparison of Net Ton Miles per hour, rail and road. I said 'what is a Net Ton Mile per train engine hour?' He didn't know. I ground my teeth.

Part of the art of management is to leave the fun of Doing to the level of authority which will get the most fun out of it. I know that the times when people do most easily what I want them to do are when I behave like the Old Man.

Out of the Mauldin stable at the time of writing (1966) there are three Chairmen of Regional Boards and General Managers, H. C. Johnson (L.M.), W. G. Thorpe (Scotland) and myself (Eastern) and one Deputy General Manager, H. W. Few. There is no member of the British Railways Board. He trained us to be rough-and-tumble managers. He wouldn't have known how to produce a back-room boy. And in that preventive medicine, bless him, he did us proud.

In 97 office at that time were Sidney Shreeve, small, round, rosy, bright-eyed: He walked into my office a few months ago and at 87 talked in his slow, rusty voice as if he were still on the job; George Jackson who timed by rule of thumb faster and as accurately as any Grapher; never faster than when he had a skinful of beer, which was every afternoon; Pip Dawson, George's shadow and a violinist; Charles Yeoman, ex-Inspector, the lad Ray Humphries and the Inspector Sam Brown. 'The 10.40 Temple Mills late away from Cheshunt? Just you leave it to me and I'll slip a bugger into 'em.' And when Sam retired, Ned Woodcock.

The place was humming. After many years of the Freight Section playing second fiddle to the passenger side under Harry Hancock and to the Great Northern under Freddie Fielder, H. C. (Bill) Johnson had arrived and set them free. He had got them not only freedom but a fleet of new locomotives.

This, as I came to know over the years, is typical Bill. He is no great original thinker. He collects round him the best men in sight. He sets them free to do their job. He cajoles, or grabs, the best equipment. And sits on top of the heap, receiving the grateful thanks of the nation for blessings such as the Euston electrification.

He has—and needs—the grass root patience of the farmer. It is the harvest that interests him. Rough weather on the way never gets him down. The progress of the Euston electrification was attended for a long time by slow timings, unpunctuality and an occasional major public row such as the one over the demolition of the Doric arch. For years I was able to make cracks about not being able to run a railway if you had fallen arches. Nevertheless, now in the General Manager's Mess at Euston is a silver presentation model of the Doric arch. It reminds him and all who admire it, of not fallen but triumphal arches. Anyone who thinks he has a General Manager's hat in his knapsack should sit at the feet of this Gamaliel.

When I came, the service was ripe for a revolution. Alas, I was not ready to lead it. In 1938 the techniques and economics of road transport and of handling goods by mechanical means were well advanced. We could have concentrated our depots for sundries and coal, much as we are doing today. We could have reduced the number of stations for full loads by at least a half. We could have designed Liner Trains, merry-go-round for coal. We could have had diesels. We could have had automatic level crossings, long-welded rail. We could have done our homework on rural railways. The opportunities which I have missed in my career ... As Norrie used to say now and again 'I can't think why they employ you'.

Over
F A MILLION
AILWAYMEN
maintaining a
Vital
nal Service

RAILWAY EXECUTIVE COMMITTEE

## 3

---

# DISTRICT MANAGEMENT
# AND WAR

About this time the Old Man sent for me.

'Fiennes' he said 'there's a job going as Assistant District Superintendent at Burntisland. Do you want to run for it?'

'Yes' said I.

'Well I'm not going to recommend you'.

'Sir, why?' The 'sir' half despondent, half indignant. I thought I was doing all right for the Old Man. In my simple error I supposed that instead of his own qualities the things Bill and I had done on the Great Eastern had something to do with his having wiped B.-W.'s eye for Divisional General Manager.

'You've started a lot of things: good things some of them. You're doing all right but you had better stop and finish them'.

For the first time in my life—and I suppose this is where the habit began, I took issue with my boss.

'I must get on' I said. 'How am I to send my children to Winchester if not?'

The Old Man laughed fatly, 'Would you like to go and see Mr. Bell? You won't get much change'.

So I went and as predicted got none. Bell had a tiny little frame, a fact that he always concealed behind his desk, but his head and frosty eyes were formidable. Both were visible above the blotter. The latter fixed me with a basilisk look. 'What is wr-r-rong with Watson's Academy?' Presumably the old stinker had been there. And I didn't know what was wrong with it except that it had produced the old stinker. It was not the moment to say so. I went away chastised with whips but resolved that the kids should get to Winchester; and they did.

Nevertheless within six months, in August 1939, I was Assistant District Superintendent at Edinburgh in succession to Harry Pallant: and pretty uncomfortable too. I shared a room with David Lamb who was Chief Clerk. David had always oppressed me with his vast range of knowledge. He did so again quite unconsciously. I hadn't arrived then at the philosophy of the work-shy that those who know everything do nothing.

Slowly at that time the English were infiltrating Scotland, not in battalions but as single spies. The Scots were nice enough about it but Stemp 'the Major' had oppressed them vastly a few years before; and the current Assistant Superintendent and Oppressor-in-Chief, H. G. Sayers, was chastising them with scorpions. To the Scots as English I was a would-be oppressor, to Sayers as English and wished on him, I was a clear candidate for a scorpion.

For murder you need motive which Sayers had and opportunity which he also had at once. I found myself District Air Raid Precautions Officer. War was less than a month away. District Office and a disused tunnel in Scotland Street were full of gas masks, capes, and steel helmets. Little had been done about shelters, lighting or training. The whole enterprise was in the hands of one Class V clerk. Scotland was going to war. Reluctantly I tore into this shambles. We spent till midnight every night with lists of staff, labelling equipment and sending it out to stations, interrupted only by the need to carry out a Sayers' instruction to inspect the sleeping car trains three times a week. Within a few days we had created a shambles of our own. The staff office lists were many months out of date. As fast as we sent the stuff out it came back with demands for different things. Sayers himself got a cape, cut for a midget. He sent for me. He wiped the floor with me. At that moment no cape would have fitted him. He seemed seven feet high and six feet wide. From thenceforward nothing I could do was right.

War broke out. I couldn't listen to Neville Chamberlain. We were evacuating a train load of expectant mothers. At 11.4 the sirens began to wail. We got the near-Mums out of the train. We shepherded them from the light of day into Scotland Street Tunnel, where they stood in apprehensive groups wondering what was going to happen to them externally and internally. I wondered too. Some of them began to be only too sure. The internal problem was aggravated by the unfinished (like all else) lavatory doors which banged in the wind a little way up the tunnel and sounded like gunfire overhead. The all-clear blew in a little while. We poured out, hustled them into the train regardless of their pains and blew the whistle. Never have I been so glad to see a tail lamp.

We settled down to the phoney war. We straightened out the A.R.P. shambles, got the black-out effective, obeyed an order from the Admiralty to dig out one wagon of mines, the 484th on the disused single line to Peebles. It took seven class 8 engines all Sunday. I got a house at Inveresk. Norrie and Jeremy and Joslin came up from her home at Llangollen. For the first time I drew breath.

We had just moved when we had our first taste of the warm side of the Scots. It started to freeze hard and thaw in turn. On Christmas Eve there was for good measure a thick fog. We were cosy in our upstairs drawing room—bright Lothian coal at 21s.

a ton. There was a thud downstairs. We looked at each other. Norrie said: 'It would be funny if that was the kitchen ceiling'. We went to look. It was. Worse, cold water was cascading down through a small trap door. As usual I hadn't found out where the turncock was. So 'I can't get through there' I said. 'You might'. And the blessed girl went. She found something to turn. All was peace.

I rubbed her down hissing like a groom. I went out into the darkness and fog, walked along Delta Place, turned left into the main road and sent a man flying into the gutter. We picked ourselves up.

'I suppose you can't tell me where to find a plumber at this time of night?'

'A plumber? I am a plumber'. This Scot came back with me and spent till nearly 3 a.m. squaring us up. He refused all reward but a cup of tea with rum.

Time and railways and war and H. G. Sayers went on. The Hun bombed two cruisers just below the Forth Bridge. One of them flew back over our garden at zero feet. Norrie waved a napkin at him. I remember little more of that time except two accidents and the manner of my thankfully leaving H. G. Sayers.

The first accident concerned a partly fitted goods train for Portobello which came to an involuntary stand on the Up line in Haymarket tunnel. The driver assumed a vacuum failure in the fitted section. He told his fireman to go back and see if he could find the trouble. In a little while he reported that he couldn't. The driver got off the footplate also. The two of them went back along the train together. They came to the end of the fitted section, the 12th wagon. They heard the hiss of drawn air. The rear pipe was not properly seated on the plug. The driver watched the fireman reseat it and emerge between the wagons. They turned to walk back to their engine.

Choo ... choo ... choo ... choo ... choo choo choo. She was away. No one on the footplate. The driver clawed his way to the nearest telephone on a signalpost. He rang Waverley signalbox. The signalman looked at his diagram. The line to Portobello and the south was full of trains. The line to Granton Dock was clear. He set the road for Granton. He phoned the station staff to warn the guard.

The train emerged from the tunnel at may be fifteen miles an hour. By the time the brake emerged she was doing twenty. The guard was on the rear platform leaning on the rail, drawing at an empty pipe upside down. The Inspectors and porters shouted and waved their hats and flung their arms to heaven. The guard waved back. He thought they were wishing him many happy returns of his birthday, which it was. He realised that something was amiss when he recognised the steep down gradient on the Granton branch. The train was then doing around fifty miles an hour. He chose a grassy bank and alighted. He didn't even break his pipe. We spent four days at Granton picking up the mess.

At the enquiry the driver—and of course the fireman, for in this matter the Scots are indistinguishable from the English apart from an even greater fear of authority—maintained stoutly that the regulator had a shocking blow. J.38's he said were often so.

'Enough to start a 300 ton train and accelerate it to twenty miles an hour in a mile?'

'Och aye.'

A bland and impervious front. Nevertheless we found that when the loss of vacuum brought them to a stand, he had left open the regulator.

The second accident heralded my departure. I had spent one night in deep snow rerailing a V.2 which had 'become derailed' as we euphemistically say at the entry to Haymarket Loco. At 3 a.m. safely on the road she set back through the next pair of points. 'Bump-rattle' and she was on the floor again. We turned to and got her into shed soon after six. I walked to Waverley, got a train to Musselburgh, walked home, had breakfast, went to bed and to sleep. At 9 a.m. Norrie was shaking me. 'Mr. Sayers wants you on the phone'. I heard my voice saying in a tone which had little to do with the disparity in rank 'Ask him what he wants'.

After a trot downstairs and back—in those days she ran everywhere—'He wants you to take a joint enquiry to-day into the derailment at Haymarket and let him have three copies of the verbatim evidence by four o'clock.'

'Tell him I'm going to sleep'. And go, I went. When I got up Norrie applauded this; she was above all things a warrior. She had played hockey for Wales, left inner, for seven years. Our principal trophy at home is her hockey stick with English blood on it. And at that a lot of blood. But I was quaking in my boots.

Next day we were off the road again. What a way to run a railway. And I was round the 'Sub' looking after it. The signalman called me to the phone. 'Mr. Gardiner wants to see you at once'. This was H. G. Sayers' boss, the Superintendent, father of R. G. Bobby Gardiner of the London Midland. I set off for Waverley, cleaning my shoes with my handkerchief, straightening my tie, squinting at my nose for smuts, telling myself with no success that this might not be where an unpromising career was cut short.

'Fiennes', he said, 'the District Superintendent at Cambridge has had a nervous breakdown. Colonel Mauldin wants you at once. How soon can you get there?'

'To-morrow', I cried. Ana I took that enquiry before I left.

The phoney war had had more impact on the Cambridge District than on Edinburgh. Cambridge was enormously busy. There was little thought then that it was in the front line. That was to come. In early 1940 we were in the rear areas, building not strong points but aerodromes. We were concentrating vast quantities of steel, cement, reinforcing rods, bricks, ballast. Whitemoor Up Yard was shunting regularly over 3,000 wagons a day. We were by-passing it with as many block loads or part block loads as we could. March Up Yard and Whittlesea Up Yards had gone back to their old functions and were making primary separations for Cambridge, Temple Mills, Ipswich, Crown Point and for anywhere else that Chief Controller George Docking thought fit in his infinite resource and sagacity.

As always the principal problem was clearance. We were working flat out twenty-four hours a day, seven days a week, for as long as the men could stand it. We were still short of engine power. George beyond all men knew his principles. You can pull traffic into a marshalling yard. You can't push it in. Clearance is all. So we were getting by. It was very hard work for everyone but it was peace time only more so. We were able, Chief Clerk Reuben Taylor and I, to find the District Superintendent George Sutcliffe daily jobs in the remote corners of the District. Poor George, hands swollen with rheumatism, eyes luminous with nerves, took this meekly. He went out in the Rover early in the morning with a batch of papers for Long Sutton or Mildenhall. He came back some time. Gradually he got himself round. In a year he was as good as new. Meanwhile it didn't matter all that amount being a man short.

Not for long though. The blitzkrieg started. Soon in our garden we could hear drumfire in the East. Day after day the guns of Dunkirk thudded in our ears. Then the men arrived; exhausted, unshaven, encrusted, numb. They slept and slept all over our house and went on. The local Defence Volunteers were formed. Churchill's slogan was 'You can always take one with you'. It would have had to be an unwary Hun that let me get near him with my pike—design Circa 1500; origin query Birmingham

Small Arms Company. In a little I had one of the three rifles and fired a shot in anger.

I had an office overlooking the up platform. One afternoon Reuben Taylor and I were there, fearing no evil. Without warning a string of bombs went off to the north; very close and a roar of engines very low coming our way. The J.U.87's wing tip was not more than fifteen feet from the window when I got off my shot. The rear gunner took no notice. 'Probably dead', said Reuben. Since I aimed at the pilot he may have been right. At sixteen I was a certificated first class shot with a rifle; at eighteen third class; by 1940 unclassified. I suppose I laid myself—and Reuben for abetting—open to be put against a wall and formally done in; for I fired this shot without first putting on my L.D.V. armlet. It was a pity it didn't kill somebody because one of the bombs fell on the accident van and killed the driver of the crane.

The Army got very bossy and trigger-happy. They erected strong points and tank traps regardless. One day I heard that they had dug holes in the main line on a bridge where it crossed a small river and were about to concrete stout steel posts therein. It took some courage to tell a fighting general—Q generals are different—to go and defend England somewhere else, but he did. That was drama. On the other hand it was sheer comedy when an armoured regiment came to Audley End to practice loading Matildas on to warflats in the dark. The double-barrelled Colonel was deeply offended with me. In order to protect the railway from some injustice or other, in aid of which he had asked me if I knew who he was and told me, I had fired all three barrels of Twisleton-Wykeham-Fiennes back at him. Stiff as a ramrod he climbed into his tank. His offended back was borne protruding from the turret slowly and inexorably along the warflats. It abruptly disappeared from view as his driver drove him over the end of the last one. It was a most satisfying clang of armour.

The last illustration of trigger-happiness came a little later. Norrie and I were getting a bit worn at the edges. I was green and still terribly earnest. Every air raid 'red' brought me from bed and into Control four miles away. Most nights brought an intruder bumbling overhead with one of our fighters wasping around looking for him. We didn't get a lot of sleep. We thought we would go sailing on the Ouse for a weekend. We hired a boat from Banhams and set off under sail for Littleport. On the Saturday night after telling Ely where we would be we moored about a mile upstream from Ely Dock Junction. At 1 a.m. the train register lad was knocking on the cabin top, demanding our return to Cambridge by 6 a.m.

It was a lovely night. The river was like bright glass under a high riding moon. Rather than go to Ely and catch a train we decided to turn on the engine and take the boat. We sat close in the cockpit, very much at peace with each other, with the boat and with the river. At about six knots we swept round a sharp bend. Just ahead from bank to bank was stretched a cable. In the middle of the cable just awash was a keg. On top of the keg was a short stick. On top of the stick was a red flag. We had no chance of stopping or turning. We charged the cable about five yards from the flag with my heart at least in my mouth. There was no sheet of flame. The whole enterprise sank without trace. The Nelson touch.

Mind you, not all the trigger-happiness was aimed at us. We too went patrolling after paratroops. Reports of their landings were frequent, especially near Cowbit; a fact which after a while I connected with the habit of March crews, when sidetracked in Cowbit Up Loop, fossicking across the field to the pub nearby. Driver Wing of March has told me recently that the practice is not yet extinct, but as trains now get a pretty clear run on the Joint line the licence can't be worth as much as it was in 1940.

Anyway one black night District Wagon Inspector Sergeant George Woods was out on patrol with his trusty comrade in arms and beer and current member of the Whitemoor Club, W. G. Thorpe. George froze. 'Deploy', he whispered. Disciplined Willie deployed. They crept on and surrounded the night sewage cart and crew.

Apart from railway work I was ex-officio District A.R.P. officer. Till he went to war Dougal Fenton was with me. When he left my disabilities became more apparent. I fainted at the sight of blood; and I had no sense of smell. The first was the real disqualification to me. Norrie used to say: 'They will have picked up the bits before you get there', and sometimes they had. The second was terribly real to C. G. Greenwood and the A.R.P. pundits, for what would the national harvest be if a man could not tell pear drops from musty hay?

Railwaymen know quite a bit about demolition and rescue. It is part of their life. About ten per cent of our staff were already firstaiders. Only decontamination was a new technique. We worked hard at it and in the suits and masks as issued got terribly hot. One Sunday I set off from home with brother-in-law Sam, for a practice at King's Lynn. There was a glazed frost. On the road between Cambridge and Dullingham a black Ford 10, just like ours, got into a skid about 200 yards away, waltzed twice across the road, hit us alongside my door and finished upside down in the ditch. 'That chap's a goner', said the Reverend Samuel Davies without emotion. We ran across. The car was completely upside down. Petrol was pouring from the tank which in that model was in front of the windscreen. We tore open the door. A policeman emerged still smoking a lighted cigarette. 'Pity', he said, 'this car belongs to my Sergeant'. We righted it and off he went.

We didn't get a lot of war apart from the intruders. One night coming back from Whitemoor by car I saw in the distance a fire on the ground which I put down as at Waterbeach aerodrome.

When I got close I could see it was an aircraft burning. After a short debate internally I drove on and was airborne for a good many yards when the thing and its bomb exploded just as I was opposite it. One day some Stukas made a morning raid on Duxford aerodrome. They came hedgehopping back over me on my bicycle with our fighters zipping them down all around. Very spectacular, very noisy, very heartening.

The London blitz we could see nearly every night. Spangles of yellow and white and red tracing the southern sky. One of the more extravagant orders—this time the Nelson blind eye was applied—was to send pitprops from Norfolk destined for Nottinghamshire to Stratford Market to be weighed. The other effect was naturally to do as much of London's work as we could. We wanted to get wagons into and out of London just as quickly as we could.

The Cambridge District therefore trapped everything for London, shunted it over and made direct loads to the final terminal. Not only that but we held the traffic until London was ready to unload. We were also the diversionary route for traffic avoiding London. Colchester—Ipswich—Bury—Cambridge—Bletchley—Honeybourne—South Wales was used to capacity. Luckily or negligently when the Colonel built Whitemoor mechanised Up and Down Yards he did not pull up the Yards which they relieved. We still had an Up and a Down Yard at March, an Up and a Down Yard at Whittlesea. Ely was half empty. The three Yards at Cambridge were little more and we added a fourth by expanding the Royal Show Ground Sidings at Trumpington. The Cambridge District shunted the lot. Ben Mitchell, Jimmy Hume, Albert Chapman, Jimmy Lord, Percy Baynes and the rest under the benevolent and ingenious direction of George Docking saved London from grinding to a halt. Nothing was ever too difficult. We never said 'can't'.

On top of all this came the bombs; high explosive and incendiary to feed the airfields rapidly coming into use all over East Anglia and the squadrons of Wellingtons, Hampdens and Stirlings which used them. Night after night they went out to plaster Hamm, the principal marshalling yard at one outlet from the Ruhr.

After a while the R.A.F. realised that old Hamm just kept rolling along. They came down and asked me why. We went down to Whitemoor. I asked them if they could hit and destroy the inlet and outlet junctions. They thought that would be far too difficult. 'Well, gentlemen, all you do is to dig a few dozen holes each night which a few dozen wagons of ashes and a few straight rails will repair in a very few hours'. They asked what they ought to do.

'Plaster the place so hard', I said, 'that you give their breakdown gangs a month's work rerailing wagons. Steel and coal are unhandy things when they're spilt'.

'We haven't got the aircraft for that'.

It was about three years later that they did just that to Juvisy and other yards. Meanwhile the Huns never bombed our yards as a strategical measure. Maybe they had some Gruppenfuhrer who had been an assistant yardmaster. They certainly had some sense.

My father had been a naval correspondent and a friend of Lord 'Jackie' Fisher, some of whose letters we still have. When I call my bosses names I look again at those letters to see whether my language has outrun Jackie's. It never has. The two of them had taught me that no one crosses the narrow seas in the teeth of the Royal Navy; and that it would shorten, if not end, any war, if anyone tried. I was therefore all in favour of 'Sea-Lion'. However, the Army too, now unemployed, were allowed a role. They allocated a railmounted gun and a crew of fire-eating Poles to Norfolk. We told them they could have the Hunstanton branch between certain hours and not to let us hear of them again. This tactic was dictated by their first formal visit to me which cost me, then a very poor man, over £3 for double whiskies. And, bless them, we did not hear any more. In this we were wiser than neighbour Teddy Stephens at Lincoln who supervised the practice firing of a gun somewhere near Skegness. The first round of the 15 inch lifted the roofs and windows out of the station and most of the village. The bang was followed by an irate figure down the road 'Who authorised this ...? What precautions were taken? ... Do you know who I am? Field Marshal Montgomery-Massingberd. Field Marshals never retire. Still on active list. Woof. Consider yourselves suspended from duty'. Teddy took this big. He had been a gunner himself and had warned the O.C. of the 15 inch crew just what the harvest would be.

Apart from the fun of all this the value was that it taught me two things: firstly that Mark Palmer was right when he said: 'Hard work will never get you down if you enjoy it'. Secondly that railways and railwaymen have a great scope and a great gift for improvisation. The second lesson was a curious one. As we are now with timetables once a year, diagrams for booked and special trains issued, the long processes of consultation about changes dragging their weary and unproductive way across the months, we tend to forget that in 1939 and 1940 we made radical changes to the freight working through the controls at an hour or two's notice, and that we followed it up with a Train Circular next day. So I learned how to improvise, how to clear or get round—mentally and physically—accidents, traffic jams in yards, terminals and lines. I have never been frightened of any traffic situation since. Apart from the humanities, if you have a sense of time and a sense of money, you are beyond fear. How long does everything take: a change of engine, water, to shunt fifty wagons in a flat yard, non-mechanised hump, mechanised hump: how long to create vacuum in a fifty wagon train; how long to unload twenty wagons in a shed; how long, how long, how long. The greatest of all is a sense of time.

It becomes even more so and takes you straight into the ranks of the prophets when you come to planning. You begin how long will so-and-so take to make up his mind—see especially the Section on ships for Fishguard later in this book and reflections on the merger of the Eastern and North Eastern Regions.

About planning ahead I hadn't a clue. That came next. Toward the end of 1941 'They' shifted me to York. There were two jobs going: one as head of a new Traffic Regulating Office for which they wanted someone who could please Barrington Ward, Jenkin Jones, E. W. Rostern, E. M. Rutter and H. G. Sayers, as unlikely a bunch of incompatibles as ever ran the same railway. B. W. and Jenkin Jones referred to each other as 'that man Ward' (or 'Jones'). 'They' thought they would appoint a diplomatist—clearly not I, but E. J. (John) Vipond. I followed him not for the last time.

J. J. made an organisational change however. He made the new Trains Assistant, me, also responsible to the Loco Running Superintendent, C. M. Stedman. Stedman was an ex-County cricket amateur and had a mouth like a rat trap. He was going to get his money's worth out of me. It is one of the twists of character that so often my lords and masters thought that the way to get me to work was to bully me: whereas a kind word and I go bounding around. Mauldin and possibly Dunbar and certainly Beeching knew this. B. W., Rostern, Stedman and Raymond did it the other way, whereupon I turn sulky, work where I choose which is with things below me and am bolshie with my superiors. This is not much fun for me and probably lousy for them. Nevertheless, on British Railways there are too many slaves. Norrie used to say: 'It is a healthy sign to think your boss a fool'.

In the current work York was pie compared with Cambridge. There was far less pressure on the military side. They were pretty remote from the war. Certainly we had one Baedeker raid. I woke one night to see in the sky to the south-west a wide red glow; no sound. 'Leeds is catching it', I said to Norrie and went down to telephone to Control. No reply from the Exchange, so I got on my bike. It was York. The 'all-clear' went as I crossed Lendal Bridge. A warehouse downstream was gouting fire. In the station the 10.15 King's Cross was flaming from stem to stern. I went into Control. Soon Rutter and J. J. appeared, a real pair of pirates in tin hats black to the eyebrows. 'Where's Mr. Stedman?' snapped J. J. Nowhere. Eventually I—chump that I am—saved Stedman by saying that I who lived near him had heard nothing either and was only there because I had happened to wake and to see the glow in the sky. I remember that I was fire watching the next night with Frank Batty and Fred Margetts and Gerald Crabtree. A 'yellow warning' came up. I was so scared that Fred cleaned me out at poker in the next twenty minutes! Scared for the reason that after the night of the raid when the fire watchers had gone to shelter J. J. had ruled that our place was on the roof.

Soon we came to planning. 'Bolero' was the name for the arrival of the American army. The Scottish ports were to take the brunt. The East Coast route was to carry most of them to East Anglia and the Southern Counties. Bernard X. Jessop was the D.A.Q.M.G. Northern Command and our liaison. Numbers of men; amount of equipment; rate of discharge at port; rate of movement south; locomotives; stock; crews; refreshments; line capacity. At that, some of the old North Eastern schemes leapt from their pigeon holes: doubling between York and Northallerton; new loops elsewhere; and so on. I did the sums.

Almost the only other recollection which I have of York was the death of Sir Nigel Gresley and his succession by

Edward Thompson. Among my chores was to be Secretary of the Superintendents' and Loco Running Superintendents' Committee. Composed of heroes all except for the secretary; and he, eternal shame to him, told a meeting that they would be sorry if they did as Edward Thompson suggested; which was to abandon Gresley's policy of big engines of around 35,000 lbs. tractive effort. The rascal minuted to this effect but the great men struck out the disclaimer. We shall come to more about big engines in due course.

York had shown that there should be planning and that there could be a logical way toward it and indeed how not to do it. However before Bolero came to us I was away again. E. W. Rostern saw me at a meeting one day in 1942 and put out a feeler about going to Shenfield which was then the Great Eastern's wartime headquarters. I did not demur. York had an enervating climate in which I was always always half asleep. To be third in a head office was less fun than being second and indeed de facto head as I had been at Cambridge. And Stedman was hell.

In due course the appointment came through. Rostern gave me £25 for the move. At that time we had no allowances for survey, legal fees, carpets, curtains and the like. At first I refused to go, demanded an interview with George Mills the Divisional General Manager. Eventually I wrongly accepted, on a promise of a large District soon. I have never known the proper tactics about money. I have always liked the stuff and spent it, not foolishly but on things like education, house improvements, holidays, travel and so on. Therefore we never have any put away. My philosophy is that an officer who is conscious of his own money is also conscious of his company's. Therefore the company loses nothing, but gains by treating people like that well in advances of salary for merit and promotion. Later at Paddington I succeeded in establishing this point and in getting in the annual review for a few people some recognition of exceptionally good work. This was in the teeth of Raymond and Dunbar who then in 1965 altered the rules to mean that exceptionally good work was normal.

For myself the £25 had two effects, both of them bad; I ground my teeth at Rostern till he retired. He did a lot of damage to my career. He took the line that I put both money and family before work. The latter seemed odd to Norrie who thought the reverse. Anyway off I went to Shenfield. The family who always before followed like lambs were bolshie. At York for the first time we had a nice house; out of York near Stockton-on-Forest; half an acre on which we kept fowls and grew wheat for them. Old farmer Fowler next door used to lean over the fence laughing himself sick when we harvested it. Norrie set her mother to work with the kitchen scissors. Well, how do you harvest two rod of wheat?

We also had Ada. My habit in househunting when we moved— and we had a lot of practice, eleven houses in ten years—was to go round the pubs. Three times during the war when houses were hard to find, I had a lead in a pub to a widow or a widower who although they didn't know it were thinking of letting their house and going to live with a daughter or a son. Whitethorn, Stockton Lane, York, was the first of the three. It came through a little bloke in a pub at Warthill. He had horse written all over him. So we started to talk about Newmarket. Four or five pints later I had a lead to a house and a choice of three of his daughters. I picked Ada. She was fourteen and even then weighed twelve stone. We got Whitethorn ready between us. Because we were hungry and had nothing else in the house before Norrie arrived we ate half the Christmas cake.

Norrie and kids and Ada had fun at York. Apart from Whitethorn's comforts and productive garden there were deer in the Murgatroyds' Park over the fence. So when the move to Shenfield came over the hill, taking us to a seven-bedroomed, three acre, full-range-of-stabling mansion at Margaret Roding there were long faces and passionate pleas to take the deer with us. Norrie thought aloud that in Essex there might be other, better deer.

What she didn't think and I hadn't thought to tell her, was that the cooker was a far-reaching black range backed sulkily along one whole wall of the kitchen. It fed hugely on coal. Suddenly from time to time and for no reason and without warning the ovens would be hot. All hands would set to baking. Jeremy came in one day while this lark was going on, glowing.

'Mummy, there are two deer in our garden.'

'Don't be silly, Jem; go away; we're busy.'

A little later. 'Mummy, they've finished one row of sprouts and they're eating the rest.' And so they were.

The work was much the same as York. Bolero was now imminent. Overlord was beginning to be a word. In the main the job was to keep things going—which were in the hands of Sidney Shreeve and Charles Yeoman at Shenfield; Arthur Edwards and Dan Sanders at Stratford; Reuben Taylor and George Docking at Cambridge. There was not much need for me. Indeed I have little recollection of what I did, if anything. It was only a few months later that Rostern sent for me for the large District—Nottingham. I objected. The thing was becoming a habit. Nottingham I said apart from Leeds and Norwich was the smallest in the Southern Area. What I meant by a large District was Stratford or King's Cross. However, as before I sat down under it and went. A trail of near refusals has been a great and enduring stupidity. The time to make a stand was York/Shenfield move. On the £25 count I had a cast iron case. Apart from that Rostern wanted me and he always had an eye for the main chance. Paul Gibb the Goods Manager of the North Eastern said this to me at the time. This is a problem with which I have been faced on at least ten of my sixteen promotions. Rostern, Dunbar, Raymond, all three think the worst of me about my attitude. I, on the other hand, know I am right but do not know what not to do about it.

# SOUTHERN
# MIXED TRAFFIC LOCOMOTIVES

## "Merchant Navy" Class

### Naming Ceremony

OF

# ROYAL MAIL

AT

## WATERLOO STATION

### Friday, 24th October, 1941

BY

**Lord Essendon**

Chairman

The Royal Mail Lines, Limited

accompanied by Southern Railway Chairman, Mr. R. Holland Martin, and General Manager, Mr. E. J. Missenden

# 4

## DISTRICT SUPERINTENDENT

Nottingham was my first full command. I thought about it rather pompously and wrote down some principles all in capitals. To begin with in the light of my relations with the Superintendent; Rostern.

NEMO ME IMPUNE LACESSIT. AM I A SLAVE? NO; THE NOTTINGHAM DISTRICT IS MY STAMPING GROUND. LET ANYONE ASSAIL IT AND I THROW THE ROCKS BACK.

NEVER, HOWEVER IMPORTANT, BECOME SELF-IMPORTANT.

BEHAVE TO RAILWAY MEN AS A RAILWAYMAN.

JUDGE AND EXPECT TO BE JUDGED BY THE RESULTS IN THE SAFETY, SPEED, PUNCTUALITY, CONVENIENCE, COMFORT AND ECONOMY OF THE SERVICE. ONLY RESULTS COUNT.

NEVER BE TAKEN BY SURPRISE BY EVENTS WHICH I HAVE
MYSELF PROVOKED.

NO ALIBIS. WHAT HAPPENS IS MY OWN FAULT OR IF
GOOD IS TO MY OWN MERIT. BY TAKING THOUGHT
I CAN MAKE THE RESULTS GOOD. THIS IS PROFOUNDLY
TRUE.

On the whole the Nottingham District was in good shape. The people who were there then wouldn't agree now and certainly didn't think so then. Nevertheless they had had four years of peaceful war. They had had practically no bombing. They had slept quiet at nights. Except for Woodford men they were not even working into the areas of the blitz. They had been working long hours certainly and long weeks. They were short of material for repairing engines and wagons; but compared with Stratford or King's Cross they didn't know what war was. Better still, like the Cambridge District they said 'We can'.

The principal, and almost the only problem, was to keep the Nottinghamshire coalfield going. The pits were working flat out. Opencast sites were opening as fast as bulldozers could zip off the overburden. Since the trainload of coal was naturally smaller than the return load of empties, we were chronically short of engines lost to Whitemoor, New England, Neasden, Banbury, Market Harboro', Chaddesden, and so on. On the whole provided we sent the men to fetch them everyone played pretty well; two of our neighbours were after all George Sutcliffe, the overlord of Whitemoor, and W. E. Buster Bill Green of New England and Neasden. The exception was on the Western, A. V. R. Brown.

This was my first neighbourhood with the Great Western. Banbury was chronically on the block. Bill Green was regularly taking such of their traffic as he could via Neasden, Kensal Green

Gas and so on, but it was not enough. I asked Brown to meet me. I expected a walk round Banbury Yard and a discussion what more we could do at Annesley and Woodford with shunted loads and engines full of coal and men to run past Banbury to Swindon or Reading or Honeybourne. Not on your Nellie. We went straight off to the White Hart for a gentlemen's lunch and home. That is why in later years in my first week at Paddington, when I went to the opening of the new signalling at Slough and saw Armand Cardani and his assistant Maurice Leach spick and span with their hats on the side of their heads drinking tea, my immediate reaction was not 'everything is under control' but 'Great Western Officers don't do the work'. In their cases the judgment was miles wrong.

Luckily Brown's assistant was Frank Dean. He was ready to have a go. Not that he could do a great deal because the principal troubles were in South Wales and Bristol and Birmingham. Nevertheless we stopped our trips from Woodford taking over eight hours waiting reception lines at Banbury. In later years in spite of, or may be because of, having been Barrington-Ward's favourite child in the wartime Railway Executive at Down Street Frank got rather lost. When I got to Paddington he was a third rank assistant in the Bristol Division, but still keeping up his interest. He had an endearing but may be malignant habit of following round Work Study and O and M teams and showing that the savings which they achieved were less than the savings which they had missed. I was not all that fond of Work Study as practised on the railways. Dr. Beeching had pressed Dr. Russell Currie on us. Russell was a great gift to work study and to I.C.I. but he didn't manage to teach railways to do it properly. Work Study became synonymous with incentive payments. For management and men it became a rat race to see who could get teams in first so as to improve recruitment (management) and bolster earnings (staff). Frank was one of the few people who would not put up with this and went round making the proper economies after the Work Study teams had done their worst. I was glad that one of my last acts later at Paddington was to sign a document appointing Frank to a command in his own right.

To have got Banbury a bit better had a good effect on our engine availability. Shouting at George Sutcliffe and Bill Green and Freddie Margetts (then at Gerrards Cross Headquarters, Southern Area Operating) did something more. Then I said to myself 'half the trains coming up the G.C. from Sheffield, Wath and the North Eastern have got on them straight loads for Banbury, Kensal Green and so on. Why put them all into Annesley?' So we started to run them up the Main Line and to change the crew at Annesley South or Bulwell. The thing was a complete failure. Out of may be twenty trains a day, no more than seven or eight worked through. The engines wanted 'a few tubs of coal'. That was the usual cry. Indeed often they wanted a lot more. One Yard Inspector looking at a bit of wire on an Austerity said despondently with a faint echo of Churchill 'Never has so much been held together by so little'.

We had also some of the new American engines. They had steel fireboxes which the boilermakers didn't like; and they had one horrible characteristic which frightened me. From Woodford the G.C. runs through Catesby Tunnel down hill mile after mile after mile mostly on a gradient of 1 in 176. The driver of a heavy train is therefore using his brake handle pretty constantly. These American engines had a brake valve far away from the cab in the smoke box. When you applied the brake nothing happened. No comforting rush of air; no grip on the wheels. Everyone in the cab looked straight ahead pretending that he believed the thing hadn't failed but would work after the prescribed lapse of time. As far as I remember it always did work. We never had a runaway. I never got used to it.

I spent a lot of the war frightened: not often twice in one day. However, one day in June 1943 I was in Rostern's office at Marylebone. B.-W. was there. Without any warning the Ack-Ack in Regents Park opened up. It made a noise like the last Trump. I jumped a yard. B.-W. at whom I was looking, never stirred. He went straight on with his sentence. Later as I walked up the platform there was Tommy Adams, loco-inspector and Lord Mayor of Manchester. 'Come and ride', he said. 'I've got the new A.2; we're doing coal trials.' So I did. When we got to Woodford Tommy said: 'Coal trials be buggered. Let's see what she can do.' Now the G.C.—maximum speed in wartime 60 m.p.h.— rough even in a coal train at 40 m.p.h.—was no place to work an A.2 up to over 90. And the approaches to some of the island platforms such as Quorn looked at that speed as if they were laid at right angles. Only once before have I been so scared in a train. That was when I was A.Y.M. at Whitemoor. I had gone for the ride down on the 12.15 a.m. vacuum to Pyewipe to come back with the 9.38 p.m. from Ardsley. Jack Neave was the guard and as happened now and again to Jack he was at odds with the driver. When the 9.38 Ardsley ran into Pyewipe the brake had a hot box. We knocked it off. The only substitute was a G.N. 10-tonner. Jack went forward. 'Thirty-eight on, driver,' he said. 'We've an unfitted brake; No. 2 speed'. The driver looked at him for a long moment. We went out of Pyewipe as if propelled by jets. When we hit the right-angle crossing at Murrow the little old brake sprang into the air. Fifty-five miles and fifty-five minutes from Pyewipe we staggered ashore, trembling, white as sheets. I thought it was bad luck on me.

Great Central men however didn't turn many hairs. One night I went to see to a derailment at Leicester Goods South. We had at that time the Old Rectory at West Leake only a mile from East Leake Control. A widower had kindly vacated it for us provided he could come for a week-end now and again. We had eight hundred roses, full range of sheds, a ha-ha, a glebe field at the bottom, a stream and little communication. In passing it was as near as ten minutes that under Nome's direction I had to deliver Bronwen. And we had little light. After the call to Leicester I went to the shed, topped up my handlamp and set off. They had a light engine waiting for me at Leicester Central. I got on, greeted the crew, lit my handlamp and put it down behind the driver. We set off. In less than a minute the lamp exploded. The driver never looked sideways. 'That's bloody good paraffin', was all he said. I had, of course, filled it from the petrol can.

This was the time of my first encounter with Tom Mead. Tom has now retired from being a passenger guard and Royal Guard at Liverpool Street. He still acts in some pretty essential roles in the office. He is Chairman of the Association of Toastmasters and is in great demand at functions which need Presence, Authority and Instant Obedience. It is an enduring and warming experience to stand behind the podium at the Guildhall when the Eastern Region has its Christmas Concert and to hear Tom: 'Pray silence' the voice is large and rich 'for Mistah Gerard Fiennes, Chairman of the Eastern Railway's Board, General Manager of the Eastern Region, Membah of the Most Excellent Order of the British Empire, Membah of the Institute of Transport, Master of Arts'. Last year I let the side and the temperature down in the interests of humility by saying 'Thank you, Tom'. He didn't seem to mind. In 1943 he was one of the Great Eastern Guards who were stationed at Newbury to work the ambulance trains from the clearing centre to the country hospitals of which one was at Cottam. Tom turned up there for the first time one dark night with a train. I started to tell him what were the moves. 'Now, sir', he said, 'if I were you I would go and have a talk to the O.C. train, while I am placing her for unloading'. He got Instant Obedience. As soon as I could at Liverpool Street I made him Royal Guard and never had another moment's anxiety when out with the Sovereign.

George Brassington now Assistant Secretary of the N.U.R. was the District Organiser. Ellis a Goods Guard at Annesley and Riley (old Mother ...) at Colwick were the principal staff representatives. Little trouble there except with the Yardmaster at Colwick, Harry Hook. I had known Harry in his days in Central Control. He had a clipped and apt sense of humour which did not always endear him to the troops. One of the girls in his office asked to see me one day. She came in, blonde, lovely figure, frilly white blouse with a ruff round the neck. She couldn't possibly tell me what it was about in front of Chief Staff Clerk John Sanderson. Out went John. Then she couldn't tell me either.

'Well, was it something he did?'

'N-no.'

'Well, was it something he said?'

A gulp and a nod.

'Well ... come ... on."

Long pause: then she burst into tears.

'He c-c-called me a Hambone'.

It was the mot just. With her frilly neck she looked mostly like the knuckle end of a ham. Nevertheless pointed remarks aimed at the staff didn't help Harry. In the end they shopped him over some salvaged barley. George Brassington and I preserved the decencies; but there was no doubt that the staff had won. Remember, you can call, and I have called railwaymen all the names you can lay your tongue to; and they will not turn on you. But before you call a man a bastard, be sure he isn't one.

Towards the end of 1944 the large District came my way. Stratfordatte-Bow: the largest on the L.N.E.R. with a staff of around ten thousand. I drove from West Leake on the Monday in our old but good Hillman through the green unscarred peaceful ways of Leicestershire, through Oakham, Huntingdon, Cambridge and Epping Forest. By lunchtime I came to Stratford Broadway and stopped to find someone to ask the way to the office. The street was deserted. There were no buses, tradesmen's vans, lorries, cars. The shop fronts were boarded blind. Even the pubs were shut. I stopped and listened for a while. Soon there was a double thud of a distant explosion. Later this sound became pretty familiar, the V.2 rocket. Then nearby on my right hand there came the steady zing and rumble of a freight train. The railway, if nothing else, was alive. I got into the car, swept in a wide and careless U-turn in the empty Broadway, and made in the direction of the sound. I found myself on Angel Lane bridge with the station on my left hand side. The Inspector directed me to the office. I walked down the platform, crossed the wooden turntable at the entry to the Holden locomotive works, turned in under the archway, up the stairs and through the half-glazed door into my room where before me Freddie C. 'Musso' Wilson had sat.

In a minute or so Frank Chilvers—Assistant; Arthur Edwards—Chief Clerk; Dan Sanders—Chief Controller and Miss Phillips had assembled. They began to give me a state of trade report. The passenger business was naturally a fraction of pre-war. The London Docks were busy with military stores supporting the armies in Europe. Harwich was full of the Navy. The northern end of the District was hard at work for Bomber Command. It all added up to doing about half what they were doing pre-war. In a while they began to tell me what was wrong. The whole place was near exhaustion. They had had five years of war. They had been through the daylight London blitz; then the long months of blitz at night; then a respite except for sneak raiding while Hitler turned on Russia; then the 'little' blitz; and when at long last D Day came and they thought they were free, the worst of all fell on them, the

V.1 doodlebugs and V.2 rockets. Every day still they were clearing up some damage, blind, senseless, exhausting holes.

They had got to the stage where men had been doing eighty or ninety hours a week for many months and were leaving their trains on the road. The engines were in a shocking mechanical state, blowing steam in enveloping clouds fore and aft. The track was terribly rough. In the marshalling yards it was virtually unmaintained. Derailments were a daily occurrence. Worst of all, the judgment of management was impaired. It was only a little while before that Control had rung up the District Superintendent at night for advice about a failure of block bells and telephones between Shenfield and Chelmsford during a raid. He had instructed Control to let a Harwich express proceed. It ran into a crater. The driver and fireman died.

Massive red-headed Miss Phillips started to take me in hand. She and Arthur Edwards were inseparable. They worked in the same office until 6 p.m. then went down and drank beer for an hour or so, then back to the office until the last train. Their output was enormous. Years later after Arthur had nearly died of pneumonia she married him. In the meantime she beamed largely on me and said two things: 'Call me Dora' and secondly, 'Mr. Wilson never gave me any dictation'. The second was surely true because for months taking shorthand was a sore trial to her.

Once again, this was a pot-boiling job. It was different in two respects. There was an immediate and stark reality about it. Holes to fill up, deaths or wounds to take care of. And of course they were cockneys. This is no place nor am I the right person to analyse cockneys. There was only one characteristic which was important to me then, their reaction to leg pulling—whether I was pulling theirs or they mine. They hadn't laughed much for a long time: they hadn't had much to laugh about, come to that; but if you touched somehow the spring of laughter, you released also hidden and unbelievable sources of energy. Season ticket holders from Loughton used to choose to stand in the brake van rather than sit in compartments in order to hear Guard Bill Moss tell me how to run the railway and me tell Bill how to get his train along the road.

We soon had a pig club in the stables behind Ilford station. Six members. Six pigs. We used for want of anything better to cut them up in the Ambulance Room on No. 1 platform. It was a daunting sight for the customers waiting for trains to see Dan Sanders practising first aid with a cleaver and a saw. The immediate point however was the cost of weaners. Dan thought we ought to have a sow and produce our own. This project came over the hill just before a gathering of station-masters, on whom naturally a District Superintendent relies for advice on all matters. In passing I can write this now with impunity since there are no longer any District Superintendents nor, come to that, many station-masters. Anyway how to breed from our sow? At such a gathering one evening I invited applications for the post of stud boar to the Ilford Pig Club. Next day I had three replies. One was a straight application. One mentioned his age and service (he had five children) and hoped that I would take into account suitability rather than seniority. The third thought it was a do-it-yourself job.

These gimmicks were, of course, not particularly funny even though they made us all laugh a lot at the time. It did mark a new and conscious departure for me. It was the watershed between being fundamentally unsure of myself in dealings with other railwaymen and being sure that although I went around debunking my own office and having it debunked by others I could still maintain discipline. It made life much more fun. There are many people who think that they must Maintain Their Position, all in capitals. There is probably less need for this self-importance on railways than in any other walk of life. We start with the enormous advantage of a subliminal discipline which we build into all the key grades through the rule book, the block regulations, the time-table, the engine diagrams, the men's workings, the rosters, the link workings, even the top and line of the permanent way.

We kept going. The news began to get better and it wasn't many months before the doodlebugs were coming in from Holland over Walton-on-the-Naze. Never have I seen such a concentration of Ack-Ack as was round Clacton and Walton. Radar controlled they raved into the night sky bringing down more than eighty per cent of everything that set off. I saw my last doodlebug stuttering along the Colchester Main Line near Chelmsford in maybe March 1945. There was a Spitfire around hoping to knock him down when he got over some clear country, but it looked as if the doodlebug had the heels of him. Flying very fast but steady at an easy height they were jam for the Ack-Ack girls near the coast.

In April it was safe. Norrie and the family came up into half a large house near the Bald Hind at Chigwell. Remember when in London it is no use doing as some of the Welsh do and all the Geordies, which is give directions by the chapels, Baptists, Wesleyan Methodists, Galvanised Methodists. In London you must know your pubs. Jeremy was now eight, Joslin coming up to six, Michael four, Bronwen one and Ivor not yet thought of. School was on us.

A few months later Norrie said: 'Eleven-plus for Jeremy in two years, is it? Then A Levels for the number we last thought of in ...' She counted on her fingers, '1964 or 1965'.

This incredibly seemed to be right. We would both be fifty-nine, if it had turned out like that for her. She went on—

'With one born every two years, exams will be continuous. There will be no good time to move. Let's buy a house.'

'£800 a year,' I said, 'won't take even Jeremy to Winchester. We can't stop at Stratford.'

'Who said anything about Winchester? What's wrong with Chigwell?'

'Or-r-r Watson's Academy?'

'Let's get a house near Chigwell.'

We set off to look and eventually saw our ideal. It was a ramshackle Elizabethan cottage in a little village, Lambourne End. It was four miles from the nearest station, Grange Hill. The post came at midday. The newspapers came on Sundays only. Blue House had no electric light, but any amount of woodworm. It had a lot of bomb damage to repair from a near miss whose crater was still unfilled except with snakes. It had an acre of good solid Essex clay. It had a pond with a sheer drop on one side, over which the kids were bound to throw themselves to their deaths but over which in the event only Norrie fell. It had an owner, Ian Horobin, who had just come back from war in the hands of the Japanese and was in bad shape. He didn't want to sell it; but his mother who had been living in it had just died. Once again as at York and at West Leake we had turned up at a moment of truth. After a month Horobin agreed to let us have it. We lived there for fifteen years and moved only when Norrie died.

I suppose really it was a bewitchment. Blue House had little to do with the reason for buying a house, which was to be near Chigwell. Our management decisions in the family, like my management decisions on the railway, were often just so. Once again let me make it clear that this book and my career are nothing to do with how to run a railway but everything to do with what fun it is to be a railwayman.

What happened next in this sequence was even more illogical. In 1946 we went down to Bournemouth to see Norrie's old Aunt Emily. On the way back we stopped at Winchester. It was a golden day in June. We walked through Cathedral and stood for a moment before Wykeham's tomb. We meandered on to the school to Outer

Gate, through Chamber Court and into Chapel. The organ was playing 'Jesu, Joy of Man's Desiring' in quiet cascades of silver notes. We lingered for a while and then went into Meads where irregularly we sat on the bench which surrounds Lords Tree. No member of Lords, the first XI, came to turn us off. Second XI went on with their match, surrounded by Wren's 'School' and the venerable stone walls built six hundred years before by Founder Wykeham. After a while we were in New Field watching Lords playing I Zingari; then in Water Meads looking at the monstrous trout in the Itchen and in Old Barge. Eventually we went back to the station and so home. Norrie left it two or three days. Then 'Can we manage just one at Winchester?'

Within two months Jeremy was at a boarding preparatory school. Eight years later four were at boarding school. After school fees and tax Norrie and the five kids and I had £300 a year on which to live. So we lived off our Blue House acre, the Ilford Pig Club and our 200 fowls. Being near Chigwell for school was supremely irrelevant. However this has been anticipating; we are still in 1945 and at war.

The end was now obviously close at hand. V.E. Day was no surprise. We dug out all the old stock and engines. We ran specials galore. We kept going all night until we had got them all home. It all went well. In those days the British nation when they felt cheerful didn't break everything up. There must have been an especial angel looking after us at one moment. We had a train stopped by signals on the viaduct between Bethnal Green and London Fields. A man and a girl thought they were at a platform. They alighted on the parapet. The signal changed and the train drew away. They turned round and stepped into space. Almost everywhere along this viaduct the drop is 30 feet. At their chosen spot they fell only ten on to the sloping roof of a lean-to, down which they rolled gently to reach the ground unharmed.

I was to be three more years at Stratford and I am not proud of those three years. It was a worse District when I left it than when I came. Harold Few followed me and pulled it round in a matter of a few months. The three years are a story of deteriorating equipment, rapid change in staff, slipping punctuality and safety, overlaid almost throughout by the electrification to Shenfield and its claims on material and men.

The aftermath of V.E. Day was predictably a reaction. The fatigue which the claims of war had not obscured but made of little account came soaking out of everyone. Absenteeism increased. Sickness genuine and engineered grew. Standards slipped. Staff days were full of hard luck stories and awkward bits of discipline. May be I was a bit worn at the edges myself. Otherwise I should then have seen the funny side of old Josh Booth, chief staff clerk, who sat at my side during interviews. He had a habit which I found infuriating of creeping round to the client's side of the table and whispering in his ear 'What Mr. Fiennes means is ...', thereby reversing whatever decision I had given. After three weeks I bad temperedly threw him out, as indeed I should have done but not bad temperedly.

I have often wondered what Josh's 'What Mr. Fiennes means ...' would have been in the case of a tiny wizened cockney shunter who fell desperately in love with a girl at Epping. Wishing to spend his all on this girl he travelled to Epping without paying his fare and was properly reported by Chief Ticket Inspector Proctor and his squad. I saw him, heard his story and only reproved him, thinking that love, of which I was in favour, ranked above even privilege ticket irregularities.

The next manifestation was twofold. One was a complaint from the girl who turned out to be securely married to a man in the Forces; the second was the repainting of Epping station in red letters over two feet high 'VIOLET. VIOLENCE. VICTORY'.

I sent him to the District's Penal Settlement, Witham, as Class IV horse shunter thinking firstly that even without paying his fare the length of journey would fox him; and secondly, that it might fix his mind on higher things than women if he spent eight hours a day contemplating the business end of a horse. For a time it worked. Then he applied illogically for a carriage cleaner's job at Brighton. It turned out that he had been to Epping. The Forces had come home, found him and had given him a hiding. Maybe she hadn't been securely married after all.

We kept on getting little spats of bad temper. One day a goods porter at Bishopsgate picked up three tomatoes off the floor and put them in his pocket. The police marched him off to Court. The staff representatives blew the whistle and the staff countermarched out for three days. The man, the police, the staff representatives, the staff were all wrong. It was a straw in the wind.

Much the same sort of thing happened in the Loco Department. Materials and tools were short. Engines long past their time for the scrap-heap were being kept going by make-and-mend or robbing one engine to repair another. The 'stopped' list grew alarmingly. The amount of work on each repair grew to the point of breaking. On a small pretext which then loomed as large as three tomatoes the fitters 'went slow'. In a matter of days we were in a rare pickle. We had not enough engines to work our suburban service. Arthur Edwards and Dan Sanders and Jumbo Williams just arrived from the Forces, stretched already intolerable hours to plan a service for the next day based on predictions from the Loco Department how many engines we could rely on. 'Rely' was seldom right as to number or condition. We began to have platforms full of waiting people, curious then exasperated, then ugly. They took Ticket Inspector Whipp at Liverpool Street and threw him off the platform on to the permanent way. There was no help to be got from elsewhere. Only the Stratford District had kept the Westinghouse brake.

The number of derailments—another straw in the wind— began to increase. Occasionally they were funny. One day I went at dawn on a bright June morning tearing off in the car to Hockley on the Southend line. One wagon was off the road, lying in the jaws of the trailing points with the Main Line. The engine still coupled to the wagon was not derailed. In the Goods Yard sitting on the base of the crane were the driver, the fireman, the guard and the station-master, drinking tea. This station-master had a habit of coming under unfavourable notice. In the 1953 floods in East Anglia when everyone else was working like beavers he got himself treed in a signalbox at Harwich till the waters abated. His wife on the other hand was a formidable and extroverted character. Once when I was inspecting Hockley for cleanliness she gave me a cyclamen with some undisclosed and possibly christian intention. Anyway on this bright June morning I demanded a few chunks of wood and some action. In seven minutes the wagon had bumped on the wood three times and was back on the road. 'Now', I said 'dead easy. Do it yourself next time'.

It was characteristic of him that there was a next time. Control rang in the middle of the night. I said 'Tell him to pull it on, same as I showed him'. In half an hour Control rang again. There was barely concealed laughter in the Deputy Chief Controller's voice. 'He has done what you told him. He has pulled it broadside across both Main Lines'. The morning peak that day went grumbling to Fenchurch Street.

Norrie incidentally when she thought the national interest had begun to abate, took a line about calls at night. For three weeks or so she jabbed me in the back:

1.  'Who was that?' which she knew.
2.  'What did they want?' I would tell her what.
3.  'Did you tell them to do anything?' Usually not.
4.  'Then the call wasn't necessary till morning'. Q.E.D.

In a while I issued altered instructions putting my family in front of my work—one up for Rostern—and reducing the number of calls at night by at least 90 per cent. The girl was, of course, entirely right. We got very pompous and self-important and incredibly weary during the war by taking calls at night which had nothing to do with getting up and out nor with remote control.

That station-master was a lesson in remote control—don't try it. However I didn't see why the Operating Department shouldn't clear up most of the derailments in the District without sending for Bill Hunting and the Stratford crane. So I laid on a programme of visits to Temple Mills by station-masters. The Yard-master, Dan Rose, a Kaiser's war M.M. which you don't get for nothing, was the best 'can' ... do-it-myself man I have ever known. Dan collected these station-masters, read them a lesson, then got a pilot to hit up a string of empty vans hard. When they were nicely on the move he pulled a pair of points in the middle of them. Bump-clatter-screech. Four or five were on the floor. 'Now watch me get them on the road'. Half an hour maybe or less Dan hit up the string again. Bump-clatter-screech. 'Now, gentlemen, your turn'. We certainly made some of them try. But the top 'Education and Training' brass of the Railway Executive whom we invited to watch, turned rather white and walked rapidly away.

1947 started badly. On January 2nd we had a disaster. The Haughley Mail, 10.25 from Liverpool Street ran into the rear of the 10.28 to Southend at Gidea Park. We killed two people and injured 46. The story comes at length because it is a good one; it is still vivid; and it had lessons for us and especially for me.

In 1946 we began to get men back from the Forces. They were good, thankful men, glad to be home and in their proper sort of job. We began to look round the District and make moves. Chief Inspector Albert Fitness and I considered the reliability of the signalmen over 55; looking at their records; consulting station-masters and local inspectors; watching them at work. We shifted some from the Main Line on to the Thames Wharf branch where the traffic though heavy was slow and the equipment was Sykes Lock and Block—the same system as on the Main Line and good too.

Harry was 57. He had a clean record; but we had discussed him. He seemed to be going to seed a bit; to be a bit slow. We said: 'He is all right with Sykes there'. We were wrong. Sykes didn't protect Harry.

That night I went home late—I have forgotten why. We were having a pretty rough time with the suburban service; the ropy old engines were still doing their best, six years after they should have retired, if the Shenfield electrification had not been interrupted by the war. Probably that was it. By the time we got to Manor Park fog was wreathing up from the Roding round the windows. At Ilford it was as thick as a bag. I found the car, swung the handle once and set off. We had at that time a 1927 Morris Cowley. It had been in a field near Cambridge doing anti-glider service for most of the war. It had no starter, very little light, and a bulb horn which we kept in the pocket. We drew it, pointed it and blew. This was generally funny without being particularly vulgar. She started always on the first pull. She was not a car to drive in fog.

Nobody else was on the road. So it didn't matter a lot when I mounted the right hand pavement, unless I hit a lamp post. After finding myself astray a few times, I put the car in a bomb site, telephoned to Norrie from a pub, and set off to walk the six miles home.

My breath was freezing at the tip of my nostrils; my steps made an infernal clatter in the pure silence. At cross roads I deliberately aligned myself to hit the correct outlet on the other side. On and on I went until the first hill down told me that I was coming to Grange Hill station. I thought I would go in for a cup of tea with the booking clerk and tell Norrie that it would be after 1 a.m. before I was home.

'Control are looking for you', he said.

It seemed a fair choice of words. We had in the Stratford District control phones in most booking offices.

I lifted the receiver and announced myself. Deputy Chief Controller Archer—'The Haughley Mail has run into the back of a Southend at Gidea Park. One moment ...' I heard him call across the room.

'Vic, I've found the Guv'nor. Get that light engine to Grange Hill'.

'Now', I said, 'tell me'.

'There are casualties. I got the emergency calls out within a couple of minutes'.

We spent a little while going over the drill of rescue services, doctors, ambulances, fire services called: hospitals and police warned; accident vans to clear the line, engine and wagons to load the debris, permanent way gangs to help with the wreckage and repair the track; signal department staff; train clerks to devise an emergency train service for the morning; reinforcements for control; information to Railway Officers who would want to attend, such as Engineers; or know, such as headquarters; to the Press, to the B.B.C.

I went down the stairs and up on to the footplate. We chuffed off into the darkness and fog. We didn't talk a lot. I was going over what I had to do. At Seven Kings we went down the local line. We exploded a fog signal or two, one of them as I remembered later at Romford Down Local Distant. We stopped at Romford for a minute. Albert Fitness was there and said we could get to Gidea Park on the Down Local. We went on and immediately ran clean out of a wall of fog into a high riding moon, shining on rail and sparkling sleepers. Except for our own chuff and clatter it was a dead railway. The high sentinels of Gidea Park's signals stood at danger, protecting the dead.

I ran straight into a moment of high drama. In the booking office a little man in overalls sat hunched on a high stool. I talked for a minute with control, then made to go out of the door. Without moving he spoke into the wall.

'Mister, is it Murder?'

'No, mate. No railwayman on the job commits murder'.

This was the driver.

The wreck was a bad one. The modern stock on the Mail was hardly damaged, little glass broken even. But the two old Travelling Post Offices not fitted with buckeyes were partly telescoped and the rear of the Southend was a shambles. Inspectors Angus Ferguson and Godfrey were leading the teams. Angus had been in the leading end of the Mail. They had got the first casualties away to Oldchurch Hospital by bus 13 minutes only after the crash. We did not get the last body out of the wreck till 2.40 a.m.—3½ hours later. There is a heap in front of you, glass everywhere glinting in the moon; on the ground crunching under your feet; sticking jagged at all angles from window frames: then wrecked, crushed and splintered wood; steel rods of the brake gear and a corner of a bogie project through the side: the roof apparently intact leans drunk and cornerwise towards you. Somewhere inside that lot someone is moaning. Do you bash straight on? No, you don't. More likely to kill him that way. Let the lot slip and settle. This is where skill and practice tell. Leave it to the men who know. Slowly, surely, urgently, one move at a time: talking gently to whoever is inside. Three or four prise and lift, saw, shuffle, prop and draw. There is cloth, blood, a leg. A doctor next with a shot of dope. The moans cease. A stretcher is here. They have him. On the stretcher, a quick look by the doctor and away.

As I went to the country end of the station I found that gangs had cleared the Down Local and had almost cleared the Up Main. Pilgrim in the box freed the latter for traffic while I was there. He had had no chance of preventing the disaster. Harry at Romford had telephoned him that the Mail was running away. Pilgrim 600 yards on the country or wrong side of the Southend could only telephone to the platform hoping to get the train on the move. The staff were of course outside in attendance on the Southend. No one answered the call.

I telephoned Romford. Albert Fitness said that the locking was such that Romford's advanced starter, Gidea Park Outer Home and Inner Home must have been at danger: and two distants at caution. Five signals certainly missed and probably seven. It did not sound good for the driver.

Back at the station trains were beginning to crawl by on the Down Local and Up Through lines. Drivers, firemen and guards hung out to see what they could of the wreck. Ferguson had got a train away to Shenfield for refreshments at 12.40. Curiously the local people at Gidea Park would do nothing to help in getting tea and so on. Now the undamaged head of the Southend left at 1.30 and a Special to Ipswich at 2.34. The driver a little revived and escorted went with it.

Meantime the Stratford Accident vans had arrived at 2.20 and started work at the country end. It was while I was watching them getting ready to start that they called me to the phone. It was Fitness:

'The fog signalman at Romford Down Distant says he shot the Mail'.

'You mean got a detonator under him and it went off?'

'Yes'.

If true seven visual warnings and one audible. This was manslaughter. I thought for a little.

'Albert' I said, 'how many trains have gone down the Through Line since that fog signalman got there?' I heard him consult Harry.

'The Southend—he had the Distant off; the Mail and the Accident vans, with Distants on. Your engine and the rest were down the Local'.

'All right, Albert, there should be two new spent detonator cases by that fogging machine. As soon as it is light go and find them'.

Two spent cases, manslaughter.

The snout of the Stratford crane was up. There was no sign of anyone left in the wreck. Hunting and his gang started to tear into the shambles. Hook on, lift, slip, jolt, crash, tinkle, dump in the wagon or on the platform. Back for the next.

I had not much to do now. The casualties were all away. Arthur Edwards and Archer were at Stratford planning for the morning peak. Equipment for clearing the line was in action. The outline of the cause was clear. I went up into the Accident vans' messroom for pints of tea and doorsteps of corned beef sandwiches. This is the time when an operator wanders about itching to interfere. He mustn't. The experts are on the job. No amount of prodding will get his lines clear any quicker. About 5 a.m. I could stand it no longer. I set off to walk to Romford looking at the signals on the Down Through on the way. Not that that was any use. The Signals Department had done so already. It kept me occupied.

When I got to Romford I found that Albert had not been able to wait either. His hand went into his pocket, came out and opened.

'One case then' I said.

'That's all'.

'Then that fog signalman's a liar'.

Not manslaughter, maybe. At the inquest perhaps a jury would bring a verdict of accidental death with a rider or two about the lousy management of the L.N.E.R.—me. Well, I would settle for that. I was too tired now to bother for a time.

Harry was not there. Albert had got his relief in early and sent him home. We had a talk about the locking at Romford and what Harry had told Albert. I set off for Stratford to arrange for the enquiry which I must hold as soon as I could get the witnesses together; then to take the Chief Operating Superintendent down to the wreck just in time to see Hunting triumphantly making the last lift and clear both lines at 11.45. 'Except, Bill, for your ruddy crane. Stop this mutual admiration society and—off out of it'. Bill grinned and in 50 minutes was gone. 'N.W.R.' Normal working resumed.

At the enquiry I got the rest of the story. Harry had seen the fog signalman for the post which carries Crowlands Starter and Romford Distant, at 10.20 p.m., come in and collect detonators and set off for his post 1,350 yards away. The Southend came down the Through line, booked to run via the R Junction to the Local, but owing to a Shenfield on the Local Harry arranged with Pilgrim for Gidea Park to do this diversion. He pulled all his signals off for the Southend. It went down a faint blur of light across two tracks. As soon as he put his signals back and took the hook off his Sykes plunger Crowlands offered him the Mail and gave him On Line at once. The Mail was block and block behind. Harry watched his contact 100 yards beyond his Outer Home. As soon as the Mail struck it he lowered the signal meaning to indicate to the driver under Rule 39a that the next signal was at danger. He stood at the open door, so he said, listening. Almost at once he heard the Mail. He heard her exhaust. He heard the strong hurrying beat of an engine still accelerating from the check at Crowlands. She was running away.

Harry had maybe 30 seconds to pick detonators off the nail by the door, tumble down the stairs, cross two tracks and get a detonator under the Mail. A more alert man could have done it. Harry was left at the top of the stairs shouting and waving his handlamp at the dim racing blur of the Mail as she streamed through Romford toward the rear of the Southend two minutes ahead. In his lamp not even a red light—white.

He went back into the box and in the agony of the moment tried to pull off his Advanced Starter. He didn't really know why. The locking prevented him. Not that it mattered in the event.

Next, the driver. He had started late, lost a little time but not much on the way. He had had green hand signals from fog signalmen. He had had one, he said, from down by the side of the Through Line at Romford Distant. That told him he was right away through Romford. His fireman had seen the Outer Home at clear. He was expecting to locate Gidea Park's Distant at the moment when he ran into the rear of the Southend. He had misjudged his distance in a matter of a couple of minutes by three quarters of a mile.

Nevertheless whether he went to gaol turned on whether he had made this gross error of judgment or whether he had driven so recklessly as to have committed a crime. In other words whether he had seen a green hand-signal at Romford Distant, as he said, or had exploded a detonator as the fog signalman had said.

The fog signalman's evidence was crucial. His story was as clear and consistent as the driver's. He had been called for fogging at 8.50. His wife had taken the message because he was out at a Whist Drive. He reported at Romford at 10.20, collected some loose detonators, made his way to his post, picked up the magazine which was in the fog-man's hut, fitted it to the Clayton machine on the Down Through, saw the Southend go down under clear signals and shot the Mail.

All very consistent. Nevertheless there was a lot wrong with the story. Guard Bailes of the Southend had seen a man carrying a handlamp between Romford and the Distant. This could only have been the fog signalman. Secondly the sub-ganger who had fogged the post before him said that he left the magazine not in the fog-man's hut but in Crowlands signalbox. The signalman at Crowlands said the fog signalman did not come to his box until after the Mail had gone down. Four witnesses within easy earshot of a detonator exploded at Romford Down Distant said they had not heard one. In answer to the question whether as the driver said he had given the Mail a green hand signal, he replied that this would not have been possible because some days earlier he had broken the green shade.

We did not accept the fog signalman's story. The Railway Enquiry found against the driver primarily with a look over its shoulder at Harry. The Ministry's Enquiry under Colonel Woodhouse confirmed our findings. The verdict of the inquest was 'Accidental Death arising out of a serious error of judgment on the part of the driver' and in spite of the Coroner's opinion that the detonators were 'something of a red herring' added the rider that the L.N.E.R.'s system of calling out fog-men be completely revised. Of such stirring stuff is a railway accident and its aftermath.

L.N.E.R

SCOTLAND
BY
EAST COAST ROUTE

# 5

# LIVERPOOL STREET —THE GOLDEN AGE

Gidea Park was followed within six months by Bow Junction, where a water scoop dropped from an engine, wedged in the truss-bar of the first bogie and derailed the train; and by Hockley where after an engineer's occupation a train went down the embankment. I was responsible for operating a service which was unsafe, slow, unpunctual, inconvenient and uncomfortable, the reverse of all the principles which when I went to Nottingham I had resolved to uphold; all except one; whether it was economical I hadn't time to calculate.

However, rescue as so often was just round the corner. It came in the form of an even greater burden. Headquarters decreed that we should start up again the electrification to Shenfield. Now the process of electrification begins with the infra-structure. You rebuild your track for the changed service and for the heavier pounding of electric traction. Next you dig holes for the foundations of the masts. Next you concrete in the masts. Next you connect the masts laterally with the crossbeams. Next you run out your catenary wire. Next you run out your auxiliary catenary wire. Next you run out your contact wire and connect all the wires up with droppers. During all this you are running out cabling for new signalling, installing impedance bonds in the track, changing all the track circuiting, building signalboxes, sub-stations, control centres, putting up signal posts, cutting back station awnings, tarting up and relighting the stations themselves. Any idea of operating a service at all during this wilderness of engineer's trains should not be on. In any event the prospect of recruiting 500 men for look-out duties, of making 50 extra District Inspectors or relief signalmen and the same number of guards for ballast trains should have been rejected out of hand as impossible.

Entirely illogically the prospect electrified everyone. The condition of the Fs and Bucks, and N.7's improved. So did everyone's tempers. We were on our way up. Now and again, of course, there were highlights. The day after we abolished Stratford Eastern and Maryland Point signalboxes brought two. In the middle of the evening peak we had a complete power failure at Stratford. All signal lights went out. After a while I went down on the platform. There was District Inspector George Gray, a Scot, and some years previously a Goods Inspector. The rear end of a train was disappearing under Angel Lane bridge about 100 yards away. George was giving the driver of the next train a green hand signal. 'George, what the hell are you up to?' George was very large in frame and in feature and very very bland. He smiled pityingly on me. 'District Inspector's Block' he said. In a few days he went back to his Goods.

The second was later the same evening. When we had got power back and resumed normal working I started for home. It was foggy and things were badly out of course. The platform even at 9 p.m. was full of people, so I got on the footplate of the little old Buckjumper. The driver opened the regulator and filled with steam, the cab already full of fog. The fireman squinted up at the tall post which carried Stratford Eastern's home and Forest Gate station's Distant. 'Two off, mate' he said. And there were two off. The Signal Department had removed both arms on the previous day.

We tore into the electrification. The design had been done pre-war. The progress was in general charge of a committee chaired by Alex Dunbar with Headquarters representatives of all the Departments. With all that the District had little to do. We staffed and supervised the actual work on the ground. At weekends and sometimes during the week at nights we suspended normal operation. We conducted everything by hand signals. Every step was endangered by field telephone cables. Every stage was fraught with anxiety. One weekend after relaying part of the east side at Liverpool Street, removing engine docks and laying connections to make every train movement a parallel move, we came completely unstuck with the new mechanical signal locking into Nos. 15–18 platforms. Trains stood at every signal back to Mile End. After a decent interval, 7,000 customers alighted and walked to Liverpool Street along all six lines. That shut up platforms 1–14 as well. What a day.

We learned it all the hard way. We were doing the first major overhead electrification in the country since the L.B.&S.C. about 50 years before. When we got to the Southend, the Chelmsford and the Chenford we did it all very differently. On the Southend for instance we virtually gave the Engineers the railway for ten months. We ran only an Up morning peak and a Down evening peak. They had one line continuously and both lines for 16 out of the 24 hours. We reckoned that advanced the date of electrification by ten months.

During this time Dan Sanders was promoted to Station-master at Ilford. We appointed in his place a tough bull-at-a-gate character, Stuart Ward. Stuart had emerged via Doncaster Control and Assistant Yard Master at King's Cross and at Temple Mills. He was, and is, a born reformer. What is more he has the truth in him, and he has an infinite charm. In those days he had no patience at all. Occasionally, very occasionally, I used to say somewhat timidly 'I think I'll have my way about this one, Stuart'. He would knock over his chair 'Well, if that's the way you want it...' The last words would be almost lost in the crash of the glass door. For the next 12 years I took care never to go anywhere without him.

In 1948 I went to Liverpool Street as Assistant Superintendent and soon after Stuart followed as head of the Passenger Section. We began what was certainly the most productive time in my career and may have been so in his. The first task was the Shenfield electric timetable. There was a pre-war draft. We threw it away at once. We started to apply the principles of speed, frequency, convenience, comfort, and last but not least punctuality. For, I believe, the first time in history we designed a timetable which achieved all those things by adding a sixth principle, later to be enshrined in Liner Trains and Merry-go-Round. 'Our unit is a train'. Therefore pick up a load at one station and drop it at its destination. This principle could not be applied strictly because we had two terminals in London—Liverpool Street and Stratford. Nevertheless we had Ilford as a single terminal. Two other groups of trains served five stations only. By this non-stop running we achieved such good stock working that our units carried as many passenger miles a day as our Leeds expresses. In later years a costing exercise showed that the Shenfield service was the most profitable passenger service on the Eastern Region, suburban or Main Line.

It was also to prove durable and popular with the public for a good many years. Stuart and I had spent many hours calculating how many people would transfer from which steam train to which electric and add in a number for growth. It was not on the other hand so popular with the Commercial Superintendent who was robbed by the rigid interval pattern of the opportunity to change things from time to time.

'I have a client' he wrote once, 'who is an important solicitor. He sees an empty train go through Ilford each evening at the time he wants to make his connection to Hastings certain. Can you stop it for him?'

I wrote back lecturing Dandridge on interval services.

'I don't want to know', replied Dandridge, 'whether you *will* stop this train. All I want to know is whether you can. Then I will tell you what to do'.

He was within his rights.

At that moment I had a flash of inspiration. I sent for Chief Ticket Inspector Bill Proctor, told him the story, asked him to trail this guy and to see whether we had an escape hatch. Bill came back in a day or two grinning all over his face.

'Well, he may be, I suppose, a solicitor in a sort of way. He keeps a shop near Ilford Station with advertisements in the window. Contraceptives; virility and all that'.

Dandridge withdrew in good order.

However first we had to finish the electrification. I succeeded Dunbar as Chairman of the Progress Committee and promptly demanded a target date for completion. The Engineers ran for cover. A good many meetings later the Chief Electrical Engineer's representative was absent. His substitute, nameless for now, sat between Civil Engineer, Ralph Sadler and me at lunch. We saw his glass was full throughout. After lunch he saw through that glass very clearly. He named the day, November 9th, 1949. We wrote it in the Minutes. It became a law of the Medes and Persians. With whatever chops and changes, twists and wriggles, we clung to it, often against all reason and beyond all hope. We made it.

We only just made it. The new signalling at Liverpool Street came into use at 12.1 a.m. on opening day. No electric train had been into the terminus. At 2 a.m. Control rang at home: 'The trial train got back to Ilford Car Sheds with the step boards on one side damaged'. Hell. We had persuaded the Ministry to let us go four inches out of gauge with them. I said 'Get Mr. Fletcher out' the District Engineer. 'Ask him to walk from Liverpool Street. I will walk toward him from Ilford'. About 5 a.m. we met at Stratford. I had found nothing. He had found one of his own cut out speed signs near Mile End, damaged and foul of the track. We were saved. As we stood there the first train in public service came up.

'Guv'nor, I want a pilotman' said the motorman.

'Why?' I said.

'I don't know the road. New signalling'.

'Nobody else knows it either'. He looked at me for a long moment. After the stepboard incident I was relaxed and on top of the world. Anyone in that mood can get anything he wants. That motorman grinned and went.

Later that morning the official parties assembled and again my guardian angel was on duty. Alex Dunbar was doing the honours on the platform. My job was to conduct Alfred Barnes, the Minister of Transport, to the front cab, settle him in the driving seat and let the motorman instruct him how to drive. All of which went like wedding bells until halfway through the instruction Alfred said: 'Do you mean like this?' and notched up the controller. Off we went, all doors still open; half the party still on the platform. Luckily the signal was off. Luckily we had throughout control of the doors. We got back apologetic an hour later to find that the half which we had outshipped had had an extra hour in the bar and were pretty sorry for us.

For a week or ten days the motormen crawled around in the Liverpool Street area, finding their way through the new signalling. They ran through quite a number of pairs of points, usually going a little too far past a dolly. Then the whole thing gelled. Harold Few went to the top of the league for London suburban punctuality and stayed there for years—until indeed some unimaginative character who in Biblical days would have been stoned as a false prophet converted us from the infinitely proven and reliable 1,500 volt D.C. system to 25 K.V., A.G.

Stuart and I were now flexing our muscles for bigger things. The Shenfield timetable had turned up trumps. Now for the Main Line. 'Why don't we' we said to each other, 'design a main line timetable on the same principles as the Shenfield: the minimum number of stops, the maximum number of miles per engine and set of carriages. Let us start with an engine, run it back and forth between Liverpool Street and Norwich via both Cambridge and Ipswich as fast as we can. Let us hang a set of coaches on it and there is our timetable'.

Promptly we came up against our share of the Thompson B.1s. Before the Kaiser's war Holden was building for the Great Eastern the B.12, a 4-6-0 of over 20,000 lbs. tractive effort as the successor to the Claude Hamiltons. Forty years later Thompson was giving us a 4-6-0 only marginally more powerful. The B.1s would want water on the way. They would want coal at each end. They would get up Brentwood Bank at no more that 40 m.p.h. and so on and so on. Then we heard that the first British Railways standard engine was to be a Pacific of over 30,000 lbs. tractive effort and was to have route availability 7. At this time engine building programmes were in the hands of a committee chaired by the Assistant Superintendent, me. I substituted 25 of these Pacifics for 25 B.1s. We were allocated our 25 out of the first batch to be built. Off we started on the timetable. It would have to be an act of faith that the Pacifics would stand up to what we were going to ask of them, two round trips between Liverpool Street and Norwich, which with the light running between the terminals and the depots would be almost 500 miles a day. There would have to be another act of faith over which Stuart and I pondered for a long time. The second half of one diagram required the engine of the 9.40 p.m. Goods from Norwich to Spitalfields, due at 1.30 a.m. to work the 2.55 a.m. Newspapers from Liverpool Street to Norwich. The Goods was a notoriously bad runner. The News was the fastest and most important train of the day. Eventually we looked at each other and said: 'The effect will be not that the News goes for a burton, but that the 9.40 Norwich will run to time'. And so it proved.

To minimise the amount of faith about the capacity of the Pacifies—now named Britannias—we borrowed from the Southern for trials two Battle of Britain class engines. We took these Spam Cans out. On the first run with 400 tons behind us we topped Brentwood Bank at 56 m.p.h. with the Can BLOWING OFF. What a change from B.1s at 42 with the water bumping about in the bottom of the glass. On another we deliberately ran down the fire till we had 110 lbs. of steam only. The fireman then hurled Grade 3 coal into the firebox for 15 minutes until it was up to the firehole door. Such treatment would have killed a B.1 or indeed any Thompson or Gresley engine stone dead. The Can just ate it all. The gauge was up to 180 lbs. and we were making up time hand over fist.

With, as Churchill would have said in a voice husky with champagne, sober confidence we took the wraps off our timetable. A train every hour between Liverpool Street and Norwich Down at 30 minutes past, Up at 45. Every other train would call at Ipswich only and do the 115 miles in two hours ten minutes. There would be five extra single runs. In spite of this the cost would be over £100,000 a year less than the slower, less frequent, less convenient present timetable. Sheets of flame broke out in all directions. Frank Chilvers came especially to see me. 'Don't do it' he said. 'You can't change our main line pattern. Do remember what happened to the last man who did. It was in 1914. It was a complete failure and he got the sack'. The Commercial Superintendent roared. 'The Norfolkman has always left Liverpool Street at ten o'clock. At 9.30 it will be empty'. In those days Stuart and I had real fire in our bellies. We both went bull-at-a-gate at the opposition and didn't draw breath until we had rolled it flat.

We did however go to work slowly and thoroughly on the staff who would have to do the job. The Spam Can trials had made the drivers and firemen impatient to get the Britannias. The stations would have to be sharper in their work, especially Ipswich in separating and combining sections. Since the Britannias would not take water the governing factor in station time would be the work on parcels and mails. We were going to lay down methods and restrictions which they would have to observe. We held a series of meetings with station-masters and Inspectors and Foremen, explaining, listening, discussing, modifying. We then went into print.

At this moment somebody told Sir Michael Barrington-Ward what we were doing. B.-W. was then the Operating Member of the Railway Executive, and Chairman of its most influential committee. 'What! send the first British Railways standard engines to that tram line? No! Tell them to do it with B.1s'. This landed up on my table. The fire in my belly was still burning bright. I sent a message back. 'The B.1s won't do it for the following reasons ... The timetable is already in print. No Britannias, no timetable'. I spent the next day with my heart in my mouth. B.-W. sometimes cut through all opposition, quite illogically and often rightly. This time he would have been wrong but I thought it was an even chance that he would. He didn't. He took one for the Southern to work the Golden Arrow and one for the Western to work the Red Dragon and left us 23. Stuart and I were content. It was quite an anticlimax when we got the engines, started the timetable and had to ground the lot for several weeks because the axles went round faster than the wheels, which wasn't so good for the motion. After that, away we went.

The only other incident of note, for as with the Shenfield electrics a good service has no history, was when we realised that for six months until the North Eastern caught up with us the Great Eastern tram line could have the fastest train in Britain. I went to Alex Dunbar expecting pleasure in his face. He tilted his chair back, rubbed his back hair with his hand, put on his broadest Scots accent and said: 'You will spoil the punctuality. No!' So I went away and put it in the next timetable for the Down 3.30 p.m. Of course we didn't spoil the punctuality because it tickled the Britannia boys pink. Also C. J. Allen. And a lot of us enjoyed ourselves when we saw our opposite numbers on the Great Northern, North Eastern and Western. Childish? Not in the least! Good punctuality has everything to do with morale. Behind every failure or loss of time there is a designer, maintainer or operator. To bring out the best in them you must set them a hard task; and see that it is appreciated that it is hard.

The next important thing that happened was that I had a bath. At Blue House we had two bathrooms, one upstairs in full panoply of hot towel rails, airing cupboard, mirrors, shelves, and so on; the other grotty, downstairs and next to the kitchen. Naturally I had my bath downstairs gossiping through the partition to Norrie while she cooked. The baths had little to do with cleanliness but a lot to do with conversation and reflection. One day I yelled to her to bring a pencil and an old envelope. I started to draw a double direction marshalling yard, an outline which has become virtually standard in Britain. Ripple Lane, Temple Mills, Tinsley, Thornton, Margam—and would have been applied to Swanbourne, Walcot and Brookthorpe if later in life I hadn't succeeded in putting a stop to building marshalling yards in green fields.

I took the envelope to Harold Robinson who was Chief Freight Trains Clerk in the Eastern Section. I believe in Committees of two, one of whom has the ballast. We started to work out a philosophy about marshalling yards; where they should be, how many separations they would have to shunt, what effect would peaks of arrivals have on them. We very quickly arrived at a conclusion where they should be, namely in the principal areas of production and consumption. Therefore London, Sheffield, Manchester, Liverpool, West Riding, Teesside, Tyneside, Glasgow would be right. Whitemoor, York, Edinburgh, Carlisle would be wrong.

For our immediate purpose Temple Mills was the obvious guinea-pig. Not only was its location right but the cost of its operation at present and of the delay to its traffic was fantastic. It consisted of ten yards in one complex. The number of wagons which the ten yards shunted was two and a half times the number of wagons which arrived. On an average every wagon was shunted between two and three times. This was natural enough. The task was over 5,000 wagons a day for 160 different classifications. The techniques of building marshalling yards when Temple Mills was last remodelled allowed in one yard some 2,000 wagons a day for 30 classifications. Harold and I needed new techniques. We went to engineer Ralph Sadler, who was promptly bitten badly by the bug.

The point of attack was the unproductive time. Already we had yards such as Whitemoor which could shunt 250 wagons in an hour, that is at the rate of 6,000 wagons a day. Once in little Norwood Yard at Whitemoor, 14 sidings controlled by a mechanical ground frame, Tommy Woodbine and Hodge Jackman shunted 720 wagons in two and a half hours. At the finish Tommy, snub nose, blue eyes, burly, in his most familiar attitude with wrists crossed on the top of his shunting pole, sweating like a bull, turned and said: 'Master, I've worked till I'm sore in the nick of the arse'. I have always thought that might be a world record which still stands. By that time, of course, the yard was bung full and we had to stand aside while the fruit trains streamed away to Ducie Street, Manchester, Liverpool, Sheffield, Newcastle, Edinburgh, Leeds. It is a fact that at the pre-war yard the unproductive time is around 50 per cent; change of shift, meal time, gaps between the last wagon of one train and the first of the next, closing roads down to make room for more wagons, and so on. We had a theoretical capacity of 6,000 wagons a day; we had a practical capacity of little more than 3,000.

Gradually the technical advances came over the hill; we redesigned the crown of the hump to permit train engines to go over it; we redesigned the bolt hole for the pilot to be beyond the crown of the hump so that the first wagon of the second train could follow immediately on the last of the first. To minimise the closing down we began to talk with the signalling contractors about more precise retardation by predicting the weights and speeds of wagons with load cells and radar. Idiots, blind crass idiots that we were, we never thought of the simple piston working in an oil filled cylinder, the Dowty retarder, which does it all without prediction or sophistication but takes not only the unproductive time of closing down but also the damage completely out of hump yards.

Harold, Ralph and I found Temple Mills too complex for a start, so we chose Ripple Lane as a guinea-pig. We worked up the case and presented it. Sir Michael Barrington-Ward threw it straight out. 'Too big a yard for the Tilbury. Give me Temple Mills'. What I have always wanted but never had as a boss, is the girl who can never say No. We made Fred Margetts, then in Scotland, free of our work. He took on from there, made significant advances oon us and opened Thornton before we had done much more than dug the first holes for Temple Mills. However, we eventually did the design. B.-W. approed the scheme. Fifteen yards became three, for we brought in to our plan not only the ten yards of Temple Mills but also the yards on the periphery such as the two at Goodmayes, Thames Wharf, Mile End and Northumberland Park.

While this was going on Arthur White, the Assistant General Manager, was also having a great burst of energy. Not long after we estabished that the Shenfield electrification was a success he began to talk about extending it. We began with Southend Victoria. I remember vividly the first meeting which I took to access the prospects. In principle the prospects of any electrification are simple. The operating economies which you derive from cheaper traction, cheaper maintenance, greater utilisation of rolling stock and crews are just about offset by the increased cost of a more frequent service. Therefore the interest on and amortisation of the capital must come from increased revenue. 'John' I said to Commercial Assistant Dunger, 'What offers?'

'£6,000 a year'.

Luckily instead of closing the book there and then I laughed. In fact, the mere threat of electrification brought us over £100,000 a year still with steam traction. As time went on the truth of great expansion was accepted. Successively we planned, staged, progressed and introduced or had started work on electrification between Shenfield and Southend Victoria; Shenfield and Chelmsford, Liverpool Street and Chingford, Enfield, Hertford and Bishops Stortford (portmanteaud as 'the Chenford'); Fenchurch Street and Shoeburyness via Upminster and via Tilbury; Colchester and Clacton. The last was with the Styal line to be a guinea-pig for 25 K.V., A.C. It made also certain the next stage, the closing of the Chelmsford-Colchester Gap.

In nine years the Great Eastern, the tram, had introduced a new main line express service; the fastest train in Britain; electrification of most of its inner and outer suburban area and the rest planned. With Whitemoor, Temple Mills and Ripple Lane it counted half the mechanised marshalling yards in the land.

For me it was a golden and rewarding time. I had energy not only for these things but also to be Chairman of the local conservative association, to be the financial wizard on the parochial church council, to go on captaining and playing regularly for our Stratford District Office cricket side of controllers, clerks, signalmen, shunters, to captain the regional Mowatt Cup cricket side, to be chairman of the Regional Competitions Committee. All this with over an acre of garden, fowls and pigs, which Norrie and I did ourselves, and of course, trips to Winchester where Jeremy and Michael now were, ha, ha, to Horris Hill to see Ivor and to Bexhill to see Bron.

It seemed to me quite unreasonable that with my bosses I was in the doghouse. It didn't bother me all that much because all my life I have had my fun with the people at my own level or below me. I can and do turn downwards and absorb myself completely. Nevertheless during the later years of this time Dunbar became Assistant General Manager at York. Johnson a General Manager. A. P. Hunter Chief Operating Superintendent at York, Royston Line Manager at Manchester and then Crewe. I became redundant.

In the mid-fifties as a result of the 1953 Act the Chief Regional Officers were elevated to General Managers responsible to Area Boards. Sir Reginald Wilson, Comptroller of the B.T.C. became Chairman of the Eastern Region's Board. He was, reasonably enough, intolerant of our departmental outlook. Departments can go on too long. Equally generalism breeds woolly thinking and ignorance. The pendulum swings as it should from one form of organisation to another. There are times when the benefit of each have been reaped and the disadvantages become over-riding; then it is time to go back to the other. Sir Reginald judged that 1957 was that time.

# BEDFORD
## Travel there in rail comfort

BRITISH RAILWAYS

# 6

# TRAFFIC MANAGER

At the moment therefore when because of the prior elevation of all the other candidates I could not fail to achieve my life's ambition and become a Chief Operating Superintendent like old Man Mauldin, Sir Reginald abolished the job. I was set the task of establishing a new office in the Euston Road to be called Great Northern House and of creating a new organisation there as Line Traffic Manager. John Dedman had already been doing such a job on the L.T.& S. for the past year. He had made a crashing success of it. W. G. Thorpe was to be Great Eastern; I, Great Northern. 'You are not to compete' said Sir Reginald, 'you must emulate one another'. This for Willie and me meant that we never again told each other what our bright ideas were. Since he had so many this was bad for me.

I am bored stiff by organisation and re-organisation; therefore got other people to do it. The staff work was easy. Vincent, the current staff assistant was equipped in every way. It was the equipment and administration which was difficult. Eventually I had a flash of insight. I asked the rather bolshie, always overworked head of our General Section, A. V. Daniels, to take it on. Danny overnight became a new man. He did it all without bothering me; he was friends with the contractors, heads of departments, messengers, tea makers. He was cheerful, tireless and rightly earned the title Napoleon of the Euston Road.

The next thing was a team. The Great Northern in its Districts was full of very Senior Citizens of whom I stood in awe. R. B. Dick Temple, my first station-master; Teddy Stephens who kept in a special drawer the letters he wanted to send to Headquarters but forebore until provoked beyond restraint; and Bill Buster Green. Therefore in a team I needed above all strength of mind. So, Stuart Ward for Operating, naturally, supported by Sidney Millard, passenger and Reg Munns, freight. Cyril Palmer, loco, an ex-fitter, foreman, assistant and then District Officer at Peterborough, tough and professional to his finger-tips. James Hancock, commercial, than whom no one more knowledgable exists. Vincent, then after he retired Frank Longhorn. A real bunch of cut-throats. Thanks largely, I believe, to Danny the place gelled from the word go.

For myself I took Ena along. She has been a very necessary part of my life for over 18 years since 1948. I have dragged her from Liverpool Street to King's Cross, to the B.R.B. in the teeth of a threatened strike by the girls there; to Paddington and back to Liverpool Street. She knows our work, she knows all our family business; the children come and lunch with her, having first made sure I am not around: she answers half the morning letters without me dictating the replies. To hear her say on the 'phone with pleasurable anticipation 'Mr. Fiennes' office ...?' is to have half your very just wrath about something on the railway disarmed; to come bearing the other half like a battle flag and to see her now in her wheeled chair crippled but undaunted and interested only in your problem, is to get in to see me talking not about yourself but about her. So I took Ena along.

The process itself of an administrative re-organisation can never be helpful to current performance. Especially is this so when the re-organisation directly involves more than one level, as this did at both Regional Headquarters and in the Districts. Regional Headquarters was being re-organised functionally into three lines each controlling commercial, operating and loco' running with a General Manager having functional assistants above them. The Districts were being re-organised into Traffic Areas not only functionally but geographically. A new area at Sheffield was being carved partly out of the London Midland and partly out of the Doncaster District. In compensation Doncaster was given Scunthorpe at the expense of Lincoln. The upshot of all this was that everyone stopped their current work and re-organised. They had no choice.

Punctuality and service went to bits in a matter of months. It is a matter of history and of fact, of great opportunity and of great reward, that the performance of a bit of railway, good or bad, stems from the performance of may be one, may be a few, but never more than a few people. The East Coast route before the war was Gresley, Barrington-Ward and Jenkin Jones. The Southern after the war was pulled out of the doldrums by Sid Smart and reverted to them when he retired, I had advanced this philosophy to my lords and masters and was called a fool for my pains. Railways, they said, *are* safe. Punctuality is a matter for Station-masters, District Inspectors, Shed Masters, and so on. It is, they argued, a matter of keeping a service going. Very well, chums: off we go. And in a matter of months performance was in rags.

I have related elsewhere that after a while Stuart Ward and Cyril Palmer mutinied. They told me that we must stop playing about with re-organisation and must get down to running the railway; and for good measure that the Traffic Managers, all bar one ex-commercial characters, would not and could not do it effectively. It is, they said, a do-it-ourselves job. After little demur I assented and re-established the functional line of control of current performance direct from Headquarters operating and loco running to Area operating and loco running. In two months we were back at the top of British Railways express punctuality and securely there.

At the time of writing this chapter—incidentally on a Sunday morning in late October clad in a pair of shorts, overlooking a rocky bay in Corfu—I am engaged on another re-organisation. Again, the Lord knows why I, who am both bored stiff with the things and who have my fun running railways, should be picked again and again to do these things. More of that in due course. Meantime, having now more authority I have refused to re-organise at the same time headquarters and the divisions. We are doing headquarters first. I wrote to the Divisional Managers: 'While we at headquarters are being distracted by re-organisation, you must run the railway. See to it'.

Dick Temple at Sheffield and Teddy Stephens at Doncaster had especially difficult tasks. They had also great opportunities. Dick had taken over the territory between Barnsley and Annesley where the Midland and the Great Central wove a cat's cradle of competitive lines. There was hardly a junction between them for exchange. Everywhere in collieries and in steel works and in foundries there was the Midland and there was the Great Central. In spite of ten years of 'Pooling' before the war and 18 years of common central management after the war nothing whatever had been done. There were millions of pounds a year to be saved. Dick naturally started to hunt them to the exclusion of much else. He managed a great deal, on his own. Eventually the lack of junctions was obviously going to cramp his plans. This led to him and Ralph Sadler and me spending two days looking at the places where Midland and Great Central were close with the idea of a common marshalling yard. We looked at the two Chapeltown branches. They did not trap the flow between East and West. We looked at Roundwood and found the site too small. We looked at Killamarsh—too far south; and Beighton—too liable to flooding. Eventually we landed up at Catcliffe with the Midland line at our back and before us the Sheffield District Line leading to Brightside and junctions with the Midland and with the Great Central there. 'From here' I said 'with a couple of new junctions we can get north, south, east and west. We can make the Midland and the G.C. one railway. But look at that bloody great mountain in the middle of the site'. Ralph rolled his head and his one eye; he waved his hands; 'Muck shifting is easy nowadays. I can take it away in a matter of months'. We decided there and then. I took it back to Great Northern House and gave it to Stuart Ward. Hence Tinsley.

Dick Temple and after he retired E. R. Jumbo Williams went on with the simplification of the railway. When Tinsley was finished in 1965 Stanley Webb and Frank Harrison were able to take another series of steps; and the biggest one is still to come, the concentration of the freight on the electrified Woodhead route with the consequent elimination of the parallel Midland working from Barrow Hill via Gowholes. When we get round to the organisation of the Divisions it is a moot point whether Sheffield will not have so simplified themselves that Doncaster should take them over. Their revenue on the other hand is the same as it was in 1957.

Doncaster were less involved in rationalising duplicate facilities because the management of the L.N.E.R. had already done just that pre-war. However, in taking over Scunthorpe, worth about £10m. a year Teddy Stephens had a lot on his plate. This move geographically was right, in principle if not in time. It linked under one management Scunthorpe with its principal source of coal, namely the complex of collieries around Wath. Later Roy Hammond did the same thing with the iron ore when he abolished the Lincoln Division so bringing the ore imported through

Immingham under Doncaster and transferred to them the slice of the King's Cross Division which included the Stainby Mines.

Apart from the geographical move Teddy found—as if he didn't know it already—that the big three at Scunthorpe, Appleby Frodingham, Lysaghts, Richard Thomas & Baldwin were in pretty poor shape physically. They were expanding fast but had done little to improve their railway facilities. Entrance E, the principal intake at Appleby Frodingham for ore and coal was generally on the block. Lysaghts were desperately short of sidings. R.T.B.'s entry and exit was a cat's cradle of conflicting movements. Teddy, at very little cost to us, or to them, managed slowly to sort things out. But coming back to where we came in he didn't look after punctuality. I remember when I was training in Central Control many years ago Barrington-Ward had started a punctuality competition. The first leg was won by Doncaster. On the morning conference B.-W. asked Fred Trotter the District Superintendent how he had done it. Fred, who spent a lot of his time leaning against the door of the Up Refreshment Room at Doncaster watching the expresses go by (with a pint in his hand) replied with some truth 'Constant personal supervision, sir'.

It seems curious to look back on but it is a fact that in other respects the Great Northern had not recovered from the war. The passenger service was no more frequent. It was slower. It was fairly punctual. There was no Silver Jubilee, Coronation or West Riding. No work had been done on marshalling yards. The great complexes of yards at Doncaster, Lincoln, Colwick, Peterborough and London still worked on like Temple Mills taking in each other's washing. Little had been done except at Doncaster, to improve stations. The main line and branches still had semaphore signalling with three position block virtually throughout. The signalmen had little protection other than the traditional mechanical locking. Even line clear releases on starters were few and far between.

On the other hand A. K. Sandy Terris had started on the task of improving the track. Most of it was already fit for 90 m.p.h. He was ready to say 100 for long stretches as soon as we asked him to do so. We had therefore a clear opportunity to do over the express passenger service on the same principles as Stuart and I had done on the Great Eastern.

When the L.N.E.R. was formed in 1923 Sir Ralph Wedgwood set up at King's Cross his own Chief General Manager's office, consisting of his personal staff, a staff section, a works office, an industrial agent and little else: not more than about 40 all told. He delegated the general and functional management of the railway to three Divisional General Managers, Southern, North Eastern and Scottish. Each of these three officers directed and controlled the activities of a commercial, an operating and a loco running superintendent. Sir Ralph did not therefore present in his organisation one of the first principles of good timetables, that both terminals of a service should be under the same manager. Newcastle was separated from King's Cross, Leeds from Edinburgh. Later still Sir Brian Robertson was responsible for worse, separating Leeds from King's Cross. Sir Ralph Wedgwood made the best of this arrangement by setting up all-line committees. Of these the East Coast Committee was one. It formulated the express passenger timetable. When I went to King's Cross I found myself in the Chair.

It was very quickly apparent that the committee was no weapon to cut through the knotted tangles of wartime neglect followed by postwar adjustment. The North Eastern in particular had got themselves so involved with their service across the North East-South West axis that for a basic revision of the East Coast we had to start at Plymouth and Swansea. Also taking a hand in things were the newspaper proprietors in Manchester. It was not that the North Eastern were not capable or willing. It was that they had sewn themselves up in a parcel. I did what other better people have done since in other fields, notably Fred Margetts with the Wagon Authority, I sent for Harold Hoyle.

Harold Hoyle, recently retired, is ex-North Eastern; station clerk, controller, freight train bonus expert, Trains Assistant, general assistant, head of Wagon Authority. He probably breathes railways more deeply than anyone in the land. He is entirely objective. He has no territorial or personal loyalties. His only loyalty is to the job.

Harold, if anyone, would move the lion in the way. The Committee, bless them, readily agreed to him presenting his own individual report on a new service. Matters were now on their way. He and I thought pretty much alike. When Stuart Ward and I were working on the principles of timetables on the Great Eastern, we made sure that Harold went along with us. He too was an apostle of speed, frequency, regular patterns and high utilisation of equipment. In 1955 in a paper to the Railway Students Association I put forward the proposition about speed that in order to compete with air up to 300 miles and with road over 70 miles we must achieve end-to-end timings between 70 and 75 miles an hour. I drew the conclusion that over 3,000 h.p. under the bonnet was essential and added 'the policy of building express passenger locomotives of 2,000 h.p. lies already in ruins about us'. This piece of destroying the golden image which Nebuchadnezzar the king was just setting up did not earn me many cheers. One of them was from Harold Hoyle.

We knew that his report at best would lift the speed of the service into the range of 55 to 60 m.p.h.; that therefore it was an interim effort. For the full treatment we would need electrification. Since electrification would take ten years to plan and carry out and since we could not afford to go on for ten years with Gresley 'Pacifies' we must shop around for a diesel of over 3,000 h.p. as a stop gap. And so it proved. The accelerations were significant, between twenty and eighty minutes, which Harold achieved not so much by harder work from the locomotives, although he demanded some, as by the redistribution of stops which this made possible. This kind of opportunity is always present in any timetable which has become dirty over the years. Harold beat the dust out of this one with firm hand.

At this time my personal affairs took another turn for the worse. In close succession A. A. Harrison from the B.T.C. and John Bonham-Carter were appointed Assistant General Managers on the Eastern Region. I was bloody wild, which is irrelevant. What is relevant was that in place of Arthur White who had been getting less like a bull-dozer than in his great days, we had John to plan the Great Northern Electrification, main line and suburban. We set John a rough timetable and then left it to him. It is a matter of history that he planned admirably but could not get acceptance for his plan. Electrification therefore passes from the story, except for the comment that the principle of hiving off planning from current operation is right. Harold Hoyle for the East Coast service, John B.-C. for the electrification. But remember to choose for your planners not backroom boys, but rough and tumble guys who will go for a year or two into a backroom and emerge the better for the experience themselves and having produced for you a rough-and-tumble practical plan.

In the meantime after the Hoyle service we must take another stride forward and that soon. In the teeth of those who will not hear a word against Sir Nigel Gresley I assert that few men have done a greater disservice to British Railways than when he proved to the Board of the L.N.E.R. that they should continue with a policy of steam traction. If ever Bill Hoole, driver and apostle of steam and now Loco Superintendent of a railway in North Wales, reads these words he will take a day off to throw the book at me.

Nevertheless Gresley condemned us to around 2,000 h.p. when we needed over 3,000 for twenty unnecessary years.

There was one small exception to the 2000 h.p. mentality, the English Electric Company. Still, now, ten years later, I never hear the high full throated thrum of a Deltic without returning thanks: thanks to the people in English Electric who thought of putting an engine off a motor gunboat into a locomotive; thanks to their Board who built at their cost a prototype; thanks to the London Midland who after extensive trials did not want it; thanks to our own people who over-rode the opinion of the experts that high-revolution engines were out; thanks to English Electric who took on the task of maintaining them; thanks to the Deitics themselves for proving the experts wrong and for keeping the East Coast service going from strength to strength in speed, frequency, punctuality, popularity. We began to plan a new timetable round the Deitics based on a general speed around 65–70 m.p.h.

I have said that planning and current operation were divorced and that at the start everyone was so distracted by re-organisation that performance was in rags. Before the new timetables I set out to do a public relations job for the first time in my life—very reluctantly.

I was now just over fifty years old. Still, except in the company of railwaymen, very unsure of myself. For the first time in his life a bumped-up timetable clerk had to put himself in the shop front. Even then probably I would not have dared to if it had not been for Arnold Quick. Arnold was an East Anglian small time newspaper proprietor at Clacton and owned with Harvey Benham a printing works at Colchester. In his spare time which was considerable he captained Essex 2nd XI at cricket, brought on the young entry and hammered the railway management. I met him first when he was Chairman of the North-East Traffic Committee. He thought he could make a silk purse out of a sow's ear. 'Take a leaf out of Monty's book, my lad', he used to say. 'Get out and tell them what it is all about'. At King's Cross I began reluctantly, timidly, to try. Once I took Arnold out on a Bank Holiday to Cleethorpes on one of my swanning around trips. On the way back we went along to see the guard.

'What do you think of your management?' said Arnold.

'They're all bloody maniacs', replied Watts.

The first stage was the apologetic. As I have written punctuality was in rags. We issued instructions that the broadcasting systems at stations must give more detailed explanations and that the guards of express trains more than fifteen minutes late must go through their trains and tell the passengers why. Within six weeks of coming to King's Cross two things happened to me. Neither of them would have happened to anyone else. They were both the negation of the principle that I should not be surprised by events which I had myself provoked.

One day, fed up with the reaction of the public to our more detailed explanations of delays I walked with a firm stride into the broadcaster's cabin at King's Cross.

'Anything about that's late?' I said.

'Yes, sir. The Yorkshire Pullman just passed Finsbury Park 53 late'.

'Why?'

She went into a string of engine failures on a preceding freight train, signal delays at Peterborough by the station pilot, and so on. I told her what I wanted her to say.

She gasped a little: 'I can't put that over.'

'Yes you can'.

'Sir it's as much as my job's worth'.

'All right, clear out of the seat and I will'.

The Pullman ran in. I gave it a minute.

Then I said smoothly, 'We regret the delay to the Yorkshire Pullman. It was due to bad management'.

I raced down the platform to watch the reaction.

It could be, I thought, 'At last the truth', or 'Sack 'em then'. In fact not a ripple on the surface. Since then I have come to the conclusion that however much the public demand explanations and apologies, with few exceptions they want nothing more than that someone shall take notice of them, no matter in what form. Now, ten years later, I can with smooth dexterity and provided I relax, divert a high level and infuriated observer of the taxi rank at Liverpool Street to an informed and objective discussion why his county is failing to develop its industry and population to the advantage of my bit of railway.

The second illustration was on a train. We stopped on the Up road at Hitchin to change engines—hot axle box. I went to the rear brake and found no guard. I came back to the one in the middle of the train.

'We shall be 25 minutes late' I said.

'Yes' with the reserve which guards properly assume like a mantle when they think they are dealing with a member of the public on his way to report them.

'Are you going to tell the train why?' No, he wasn't.

'Have you seen the Line Traffic Manager's instructions that you should?'

'Yes; the Line Traffic Manager's not my guv'nor. Mr. 'Uskisson's my boss'.

'Well, I'm the Line Traffic Manager ...' We began to negotiate a settlement and in a short time arrived at a proper democratic conclusion that he would do the front half of the train and I would do the rear half. I set off, opening compartment doors, 'The British Transport Commission regret that ...' A lot of people looked up, a lot more didn't. A few nodded, a few glared; one bloke snarled; one said 'Thank you'.

The last compartment in the train was full of enginemen travelling home on the cushions. I admit I hesitated. Then I thought why not, let's see what happens. I flung back the sliding door. 'Gentlemen, the British Transport Commission regret to announce that the engine has had a hot axle box. It has had to be changed. We expect to be 28 minutes late at King's Cross'. There was a complete hush. I stood there with, I hope, the look on my face of a public servant carrying out an unpleasant duty with calm resolution. On their side I could hear the wheels going round in their heads. 'Who is this guy? ... is he a railwayman? ... if he is, is he taking the mickey out of us?' Which I suppose I was. Finally the senior driver dealt with the situation. He put on a frog-like expression and said 'Guv'nor, what is a hot axle box?' You get, you know, from being a railwayman some very jolly rewards.

Spurred on by Arnold, aided and abetted by Frank Longhorn the next thing was a tour of the line in full dress with special train. We took the saloon; we attached an old cinema coach, with at the end where the screen normally was, not the Travel Game nor How to Manage with a Computer, but me. We took with us the Chairmen and Secretaries of our four Sectional Councils; No. 1. Salaried, No. 2. Enginemen, No. 3. Traffic Grades, No. 4. Terminal. We stopped for an hour at each principal place where we were met by the Local Departmental Committees. I made a speech at them for 20 minutes. They had 40 minutes at me. Then off to the next.

The object was in essence a recruiting drive. The theme was the security of the Great Northern. In this we had a good deal to talk about. The Hoyle timetable offered more trains to work. We were about to introduce the Master Cutler. The Suburban timetable had an increased frequency. Freight traffic was increasing fast at Scunthorpe and more slowly but significantly at Sheffield and in the coalfields. We needed more men and good men. Arnold curiously was right. Within a month for instance Mexboro' was up to strength.

I made 23 speeches in three days and had fun with the questions and answers. The Sectional Council representatives who heard all

23 had less fun. One of my illustrations about recruitment of good men rather than the dregs of the nation was a written character we had just had from a Headmaster. It read: 'A Polish Jew. His wartime experiences no doubt account for his being both defiant of and subservient to authority ... speaks with a pronounced lisp and walks with a limp ... suitable for British Railways'. I used to thunder on about the Headmaster until on the third day Albert Goldfinch of King's Cross came up to me and said in his slow warm grinding voice 'Look, Guv'nor, this Polish Jew of yours. I've had him. Either he leaves the train or I do'. Albert stayed.

It was only last year that I paid Albert back for that because I was very fond of that Polish Jewboy. Richard Hardy, that determined stoker of Chapelon Pacifics between Calais and Paris and in his spare time Divisional Manager at King's Cross, has once every six months a meeting of his Staff representatives for a 'State of the Union' message from him. He does this very well indeed. There are few managers of men as good as Richard. He invites me to go along; and I go when I can for the fun of hearing Richard doing his stuff.

One meeting was enlivened by a prolonged argument between Gregory representing King's Cross Parcels and Albert Goldfinch representing King's Cross Goods. In a short time both were on their feet at the same time, both shouting the odds at each other. Richard could get neither to sit down. Eventually I said very slowly: 'I don't know whether Greg or Albert is right, but I do know how to solve their problem. We have just passed an Act about Homosexuality. Let us shut Greg and Albert up in a bedroom and see whether when we let them out they are consenting adults'. There was a moment's hush; then the laughter came. Shout after shout. Before it had finished Greg and Albert were down. Richard went on with the next business. I reflected I had come a long way in confidence about handling audiences in ten years.

The other principal event for me at King's Cross was that after 30 years on the railway I came to terms with the front end. At Whitemoor I had started badly with Harold Few's father. Driver Few was an Alderman of Cambridge, an exalted personage both by rank and by his elevation of seven feet or so above me on the footplate. I saw no reason why those advantages should prevent him getting off the Tank road across to the Up Yard and away with his train back to Cambridge to time. It became a war which he won with insolent ease. From then on for me there was always a generic adjective, the 'bloody' loco.

At King's Cross for the first time I inherited the Gresley middle big end and a failure on an express every day; often more than one. I inherited also Driver W. Hoole. Bill and I made a bad start. In the first month or so we had two cases, one a bomb hoax, in which Bill had been badly late away from King's Cross and had made up 20 or 30 minutes to Doncaster. I wondered whether Bill did it on purpose for the fun of going on the tear. Then one morning I noticed in the Express Freight record a tiny sentence '266:5 Grove Road W/c Talisman'. Now 266 was our 3.15 p.m. Flying Freight to Scotland but she didn't ever, couldn't ever, shouldn't ever run down the Talisman. I found that again this was Driver Hoole. He had been 23 minutes late from King's Cross Goods after an argument with his injectors. He had then the 3.40 Leeds express two minutes behind him and the Talisman with only eight coaches, 22 behind. On 266 Down he had 47 wagons around 450 tons and the usual Pacific diagrammed to work back from Newcastle with the breakfast car train next morning. Bill set off and by the time he had got to Hitchin, 30 miles out, the 3.40 was well astern. He then squared his shoulders and ran the 27 miles to Huntingdon in 20 minutes dead, at an average speed of 75 miles an hour. They stopped him there for a hot axlebox on a wagon, and no wonder. Bill took his train gently into Peterborough, detached the wagon in Westwood Yard, and was up at the outlet signal whistling. The signal remained at danger, not only while the 3.40 went by but also the Talisman. Then the board came off and Bill opened the regulator. The Talisman averages nearly 80 miles an hour beyond Peterborough. It took Bill nearly to Retford to run him down. I began to have doubts about safety.

However one of the chores which at the outset I took on most reluctantly was to be Chairman of No. 2 Sectional Council, the regional appeal court for the enginemen. I knew little or nothing about enginemen's agreements and I did my homework top, bottom and sides for weeks before the first meeting; for I knew also that they would possibly resent, certainly watch like hawks the first non-technical man who had taken the chair at their Council. I hadn't been in the first meeting for many minutes before I knew that I was in the presence of quality such as we haven't in any other part of the railway. With Terry Miller, Cyril Palmer and Frank Longhorn around I got by all right and began to have fun with them.

The Chairman of the Staff Side, Ernest Porter of March, I had known only slightly for some years. It is different now. Two or three times a year the two of us settle down quite irregularly and talk over the state of the nation. The secretary, Leslie Renshaw of Lincoln, able, well-documented, tenacious. Big Bill Doughty of Doncaster, whose son is a University lecturer and is himself now an instructor at our Ilford School. Someone had told me to be wary of Bill and I was wary for a month or two. Then one day at our Summer meeting in the Miners' Holiday Camp at Skegness I was walking up a corridor behind Bill. He was crooning under his breath an old favourite of Norrie's:—

My baby has gone down the plug 'ole;
My baby has gone down the plug.

The poor little thing
Was so skinny and thin
It oughter bin barfed in a ju-hug.

I stopped being wary there and then and have been greatly
rewarded over the years for doing so. Albert ('There'll-be-Trouble-
at-Darnall-Mr. Fiennes') Wild. Joe Andrews and Dick Brock of
Stratford. Dick was a tough contestant. Cyril Palmer and I got
alongside him after one meeting when we had a complaint from
Millhouses men about the noise in Kentish Town Hostel, where
they couldn't sleep and rather than work trains back exhausted and
unsafe they travelled home passenger. I said to Ernest Porter 'Let's go
there and see for ourselves'. So they deputed Dick Brock. Cyril, Dick
and I went down for an evening meal; then we settled to snooker.
The pints came and went. At 11 p.m. we switched off what had
become almost gales of laughter and went to bed. None of us heard
a sound all night. At the next meeting—'Complaint not sustained'.

I took to riding on footplates a fair amount. When we got the
prototype Deltic with Bill Hoole in the seat we went over Stoke
summit at 91 m.p.h.; after having been checked twice between
Tallington and Corby for no other reason than that we were
running ahead of the block bells. I stood on the footplate of that
Deltic at 106 m.p.h. drinking a cup of tea as steady as a rock. I
was behind Barringer of Doncaster when he accelerated from a
'7 bell' stop at Arlesey to 103 m.p.h. in seven miles. I went to open
the new cricket ground at Colwick and on the way back clocked
91 m.p.h. down Stoke Bank behind a Class 9 Freight engine with
only a 5ft. 3in. wheel. I talked to Chief Mechanical Engineer Freddie
Harrison, Terry Miller, Cyril Palmer about whether the nuts and
bolts would fall off; to Cyril, Colin Morris, Ernest Porter, Bill
Doughty. I came to the conclusion that the top link men at King's
Cross, New England, Grantham and Doncaster (the last after we

had made some changes in the top link) knew very precisely what they were up to. We need have no doubts about safety. We need have no doubts about morale. Provided we gave them the tools, the harder we pushed them, the harder they would go and so it proved.

The rest of my time at King's Cross is a blur. Norrie was dying. In 1955 she had had a minor operation for a mole on her stomach. We were told that if we had no trouble for a year we were safe. We made the year. In less than a month after she found a lump and went into hospital for a really rough operation. We were told that they had done everything they could. It would now be a 'miracle' if it did not recur and if it did there was nothing more to be done. Norrie fought her way back to full activity and for more than three years we thought we were all right. In the summer of 1960 she began to be in pain. In the autumn we went for a short holiday to her home in Llangollen and on to Bangor where she had been at University and had begun to play international hockey and tennis. Then home and into hospital.

They tried the new cytotoxic drugs but brought her blood count down quickly and dangerously. From then all they could do was to keep her as comfortable as drugs could until she died. In this they did a grand job. She gradually withdrew from the world. For three months I went in mornings on the way to work. I left Great Northern House after lunch and spent four or five hours with her. With her in the room unable to talk it out with her or with our young family never could I have imagined such loneliness.

At the office Ena and Stuart and Cyril and Freddie Wright who had replaced James Hancock, took everything completely off my shoulders. They offered no sympathy which would have been intolerable, only a steady cheerful practical approach to the problems. On December 22nd Norrie died quietly with her hand in mine. After the formalities I went home. I heard keening. I saw visions. I was pretty far round the bend.

Sensibly, as I now think, I said to myself 'What you are feeling cannot be grief. The time for that is over. It is self-pity and self-pity is a rotten way of life. Snap out of it'. So after Christmas Michael and I went off for ten days hard exercise in Devon. And then I started afresh.

What I had to start afresh with was no fun at all. It was to meet the re-organisers all over again. Sir Reginald Wilson having abolished the departmental and District Officers and set up the three Line Traffic Managers and Area Traffic Managers in their stead, then turned loose a committee to report on the new organisation. The Committee was of three. Medwyn Ormerod now Chairman of Batchelors, a subsidiary of Unilever; Peter Ricardo of I.C.I. and one of our own Traffic Managers, Dick Temple.

They were bound to report in favour of one or two things: either that the General Manager should stop building his own departmental empire with an Assistant General Manager (Commercial) an Assistant General Manager (Works & Planning) with more to come; or that the Lines should be abolished. Predictably they reported the latter. My last months in 1960 at King's Cross were spent with Willie Thorpe and John Dedman defending the positions which Sir Reginald had set up at such cost only three years before.

I reflect now that pre-war the L.N.E.R. set up an organisation in 1923. It stood the test of time, give or take a little, until 1947. Since then I have been re-organised in 1948–9, 1953, 1955, 1956–7, 1960, 1962, 1964, 1966–7. I reflect firstly, as A. P. Hunter says, people should make up what minds they have; secondly that for British Railways it is, to use the mildest term I know, not so good.

# 'ALL-IN' HOLIDAYS IN
# SCOTLAND

*from*

# 14 *gns.*

## APPLY FOR DETAILS TO YOUR LOCAL TRAVEL AGENT OR RAILWAY STATION

*ARRANGED BY THE CREATIVE TOURIST AGENTS' CONFERENCE IN ASSOCIATION WITH BRITISH RAILWAYS*

# 7

# CHIEF OPERATING OFFICER B.R.

Anyway before any conclusions were reached or action taken, I found myself as Chief Operating Officer at the British Railways Board, reflecting on Robin Oakapple's comment on the portraits of his interfering ancestors in Ruddigore 'I will give them all to the nation and no one shall ever look upon their faces again'. Soon afterwards the moves to abolish the Eastern Region Lines began. On the London Midland 'Lines' were set up. It is interesting that the same people should have done both.

John Vipond had just retired from Chief Operating Officer. He was the fully-equipped 'Organisation Man'. Diplomatic, well informed, excellent at communications. John had friends everywhere on the railway and in industry. He and Harold Hoyle recently transferred from Liverpool Street were a well-matched team.

I could not play the hand in John's way for reasons which should already have become obvious in this account. After a fortnight, Ena and I added up the score. The average number of sheets of paper through her to me each day was 292. The number of days on which I should be sitting on a Committee was 212 out of the next 250. My idea of what I was there for was firstly to get new ideas for transport by rail; secondly to develop those ideas up to the point of but not beyond proving their feasibility; thirdly to act as a spur to good performance by the Regions. Contrariwise I was not there to be an operating manager or I would have had that title.

We got the paper down to around 50 pieces a day; and the Committees to 50 days by delegation, combination, resignation. The only trouble we had was with the Staff Suggestions Committee. 'Top people must sit on the Staff Suggestions Committee. This is essential to Internal Relations'. Now I know the kind of people who put in suggestions and make quite a good living out of it. Therefore I had no compunction in telling the secretary that when they wanted my advice or presence on a particular suggestion he could ask for it. He never did.

The other thing which I had to get straight was Traffic Adviser Raymond's habit of having the Chief Operating Officer at his morning Commercial letter-opening with his officers. This often developed into a witch-hunt about current detailed operating performance. As a start I tried to give the answers, then I began to tell him that it wasn't what we were there for. Then I stopped going to the letter-openings. It didn't endear me to him. It should have been clear by now that if there is one characteristic which I enjoy it is the ability to get across my boss and 222 Marylebone Road was full of bosses, actual or would-be. The only exception to this was Dr. Beeching. To cross him I would never dare, nor want.

To begin with he oppressed me vastly with his intellectual gianthood. In his presence I was tense, tongue-tied and often plumb stupid. He was as relaxed as they come. When I went to see him I was the one person he wanted to see; the subject I wanted to talk about was the only one in which he was interested; and he had all the time in the world. All of those propositions were untrue but warming. Gradually I relaxed too. Now I know that

Old Man Mauldin and he are the only two people for whom I would gladly go back to work.

Whether he would 'accept the slave' is an open question. It is seldom on a railway that we get our characters written and then generally by mistake. The reports from our Staff Colleges at Woking and Derby are Top Secret. The annual appraisals have a limited circulation. For instance I wonder but do not know what my mark is in the column headed 'Co-operation'. Nevertheless I got my character from him. Durham University asked him to go and talk to them about the future of the railway. He told me to go in his place. The draft letter read 'Mr. Fiennes has a deep understanding of our problems'. This last sentence was expunged in green ink and in its place was written: 'Mr. Fiennes has a long experience of railways'. I taxed him with this in a speech at a Western Region's Golf Dinner last year. He laughed and said he never used green ink.

Having with Ena cleared the decks of most of the paper and the ruck of the Committees and with all my experience and ignorance of the problems on my head I had time to think. It is one of the disasters about British Railways that in the years between 1947 and 1955 no one had done the basic work on what we were there for at all; what traffic should be carried by what methods in what quantities, where from and to, at what rates. The upshot was that the Modernisation Plan produced in 1953–55 with the support of the Government to the extent of £1,500m. was little more than a change from steam traction plus a host of mouldering schemes which the B.T.C. and the Regions had found after a hurried search in their pigeon holes. We had made the basic error of buying our tools before doing our homework on defining the job.

The first task seemed to be to stop one thing which was already well advanced: marshalling yards. The nation by accepting the Modernisation Plan had willed a national plan for marshalling yards costing £85m., enough to build between 20 and 30 yards. The Eastern Region were well ahead planning Temple Mills, Ripple Lane, Tinsley: the North Eastern with Tyne, Tees, Healey Mills and Stourton: the London Midland with Swanbourne and Carlisle; Scotland with Thornton, Perth and Millerhill; the Western with Margam, Brookthorpe and Walcot; the Southern with Tonbridge.

Did we need marshalling yards at all? I remember Ralph Wilson the Cartage Manager at Liverpool Street arguing in about 1950 that the future lay in full train loads for everything; and that any sorting should be done not with the wagon but with the body, that is to say by crane in what we now call Liner Train Depots. This philosophy was being reviewed now by some of the new men at the B.R.B. I did some quick sums. We were carrying some 250m. tons of traffic a year. Of this we might get 130–140m. in full train loads of firstly coal for electricity, gas, industry and for domestic coal concentrations; secondly, of iron ore, dolomite, limestone and semi-finished steel; thirdly, of the growth traffics of oil, cement, fertiliser, grain, motor cars. May be 10–12m. tons of general merchandise would transfer from the network of express freight trains to the Liner Trains. That left 90–110m. tons of traffic. Should we throw it away, as one bandwagon full of cheering nihilists wanted? Should we go back to Ralph Wilson and accept nothing by rail except in full train loads or in containers? If so, what must the container depots look like? What happened to Private Sidings? Why, if the container transfer philosophy was right, did all the costing exercises show that traffic between Private Sidings was profitable even though passing through marshalling yards and carted traffic was not? These were a few of the questions which I asked following the distinguished precedent of Socrates. The similarities between us were that we both knew the answers before we asked the questions. The difference was that as a reward he got a bowl of hemlock: I got eventually kicked upstairs to Paddington. Meantime the questions were too difficult for the opposition. They folded their tents.

Having established by default the principle that we needed marshalling yards, the next question was where? If you look at the lists of prospects you will see that there were two schools of thought about location. The Harold Robinson-Fiennes principle of locating in the principal areas of production and consumption; and the green fields people: thus:—

| | |
|---|---|
| *P & C areas:* | Temple Mills, Ripple Lane, Tinsley, Tyne, Tees, Healey Mills, Stourton, Thornton. |
| *Greenfields:* | Swanbourne, Carlisle, Perth, Millerhill, Margam, Brookthorpe, Walcot. |

Of the former Arthur Dean rightly stopped Stourton because he foresaw such a rationalisation in the cross-Pennine routes that Healey Mills and Tinsley between them could tackle the West Riding and South Yorkshire. Of the latter I was too late to stop Carlisle, Perth, Millerhill and Margam. I did stop Swanbourne, Brookthorpe and Walcot. The Bletchley flyover remains as a memorial to the people who failed to see that railways must live by concentration and not dispersal. We had, Stuart Ward and I, indeed driven from Great Northern House a pretty big nail into Swanbourne's coffin by refusing to put into it any East Coast traffic. From that moment the writing was on the wall. Swanbourne should have been stopped then.

It was not so easy—and I didn't try all that hard—to activate the schemes which were obviously right. There should be a yard in Glasgow, but Perth, Millerhill and Carlisle just being built would die if there were. There should be good yards at the northern and southern end of the industrial complex in Lancashire, but we had not yet done our homework on which main lines were to be developed into Lancashire. The same was true of South Wales, Margam just opened was clearly wrong. It was not calculable at that moment whether Newport or Bristol was right. However in the Black Country the London Midland were beginning to work on a project for Bescot. Harold Robinson had just died, alas, but he would have approved.

I therefore threw my weight against authorising any new projects for marshalling yards, unless they were in a principal area of production and consumption and as generally went without saying, the routes to them were secure. The next and urgent thing was to do what should have been done in 1947, to begin a study on which routes would continue. We got red-headed Henry Sanderson up from District Operating Superintendent, Glasgow, to do this work. The bandwagon of nihilists uttered loud cries of joy. For a while not only no traffic but no piece of railway was safe from them. Luckily Freddie Margetts had recently arrived as Operating Member of the Board. Dr. Beeching and he had got themselves involved up to the neck with the Minister of Transport about unremunerative railways, by which for the moment they meant branch lines. So the bandwagon too took the junction to the branch.

From this I stood aloof. To me as Chief Operating Officer it mattered not very much whether we ran a passenger service between the Main Line and say, St. Ives, Fowey, Looe, Aldeburgh, Mablethorpe, Hornsea or Caernarvon. These were social problems and should be settled politically. On the other hand it mattered enormously that we should get our structure of Main Lines right not only because each talked in millions of pounds a year for operation and maintenance but in many millions of capital for marshalling yards, motive power depots, freight terminals, signalling and the rest. So Henry Sanderson aided and abetted by some under-cover agents in the Operational Research and costing offices set out to close the Great Central Main Line from somewhere around Killamarsh to the border of the London commuter area. This was clearly right. He set out also to study the five routes across the Pennines and the three routes to Scotland, about which there were no immediately obvious answers. I shall be telling the story later how after I went to Paddington James Ness inherited this work and what happened to it then.

From these last pages it will have been obvious that I had been thinking about the wagon as a necessary evil for which we had to have a few large marshalling yards where the wagons originated or terminated in consignments of less than train loads. It followed that the train load was also in the forefront of much thought. It followed also from the change of traction that the train load would firstly be much larger, no longer 250–800 tons but 1,000–2,000 tons as a first step; and secondly that it could consist not just of wagons but of one integral unit of a locomotive and wagons. The electric or diesel locomotive would not be taking water at every change of direction nor need it be inspected for fallen arches.

In a bath I started on the sums about merry-go-round. Freddie Gray was a principal and stout ally in the costing service. I put to him some basic examples of a 1,300 ton train shuttling back and forth between a colliery and a power station, barely hesitating under bunkers to load, not stopping at all to unload. Freddie came up with direct costs plus an average contribution to system costs of around one halfpenny per ton mile. We were charging for power station coal around 2½d. to 4d. and for iron ore anything from 3d. to 11d. Merry-go-round was an obvious winner.

Let me explain here why 'merry-go-round'. In a little while we shall come to Liner Trains. In the meantime the title Liner made me spit blood. To hell with Ocean Liners and to hell with 'our good friends the shipping companies' too. Who thought of running to time? not shipping. Who until the air boys arrived were the most unpredictable form of transport? The greatest compliment we can pay to anything for speed and reliability is to compare it with a train. I will call my bit of homework Merry-go-Round. It will to some extent debunk the Liner Train. The Public Relations Department were out of sympathy. Over the article in which I took the wraps off Merry-go-Round the Editor wrote ponderously 'Trains in Circuit'. Soon afterwards 'Merry-go-Round' stuck.

It stuck as a title. To translate it into equipment was far more difficult. From the railways it required locomotives of the largest size; it required new wagons fitted for automatic discharge while still on the move; it required a precision of operation which was foreign to the happy-go-lucky characters who work coal trains in, for instance, South Yorkshire. Far more difficult than that Merry-go-Round required a re-design and re-equipment of both terminals of the journey, neither of which was owned by the railway. At the loading end there would be in the case of coal, the National Coal Board; in the case of iron ore either the British Transport Docks Board or one of the Steel Companies, in the case of sugar the British Sugar Corporation or Tate & Lyle, and so on. At the unloading end there would be the Central Electricity Generating Board or a Steel Company or a sugar store. The cost of re-equipment would not be inconsiderable, upward of £250,000 for each terminal. There were some long faces at the Board.

Then we had a bit of luck. Harold Hoyle was working on a case which Scotland had submitted for 550 new 24½ ton hopper wagons, to run between a new colliery Monktonhall near Edinburgh and a new power station at Cockenzie. We re-did the sums on the basis of Merry-go-Round. The number of wagons needed was not 550 × 24½ tons but 44 × 32½ tons. If there is one thing more than another which the Board like to do it is to turn down a case for new wagons. We had no trouble. Off we went with the N.C.B.

and G.E.G.B. and in a matter of months the plans were redrawn. Merry-go-Round was in orbit.

The next stage also was marked by conviction. After a matter of not more than three or four meetings the C.E.G.B. agreed to design all their new base-load coalfired power stations for Merry-go-Round—West Burton, Cottam, Eggborough, Ferrybridge, Fidlers Ferry, and so on, and that where a re-design of stations under construction or already built was possible they would do this also—Thorpe Marsh, Drakelow C, and so on. We had in prospect within seven years merry-go-round for some 60m. tons of electricity coal. A new agreement on charges took account of the greater productivity of the railway. From now neither road nor water nor pipeline could stand up to us.

At the loading end we were less clever. The N.C.B. agreed to design two new collieries for rapid loading through bunkers. Monktonhall aforesaid and Bevercotes in the Eastern Region. Then we ran foul of a cross current which swept us away with it for five whole years. The great and good Doctor was rightly critical of our enormous fleet of wagons. Some types made no more than 20 journeys a year. At no type and at no aspect of that type's operation did he gnash his teeth more frequently and more loudly than at the mineral wagon and its habits for standing for most of the summer doing nothing at all and for a not inconsiderable part of the winter in sidings at collieries waiting to be loaded and labelled. The capital sum involved in these wagons was around £400m.

'You shall pay for this' said Dr. B. to Lord Robens. 'Ten million pounds a year and cheap at the price'.

'What?' said Lord Robens, 'And pay as well to re-equip most of my long-life collieries with bunkers for your blasted merry-go-round. No, Sir!'

In vain I argued that their argument was unreal. It was a paper transfer from the pocket of one nationalised industry to another; whereas my case was not only one of a direct and solid contribution to the productivity of both industries, let alone the nation. Merry-go-Round in itself would reduce the fleet of mineral wagons from around half a million to 100,000. It was no use. Five years.

There are of course two people in an argument. One is the person who is not convinced. The other is the person who fails to convince him. If the outcome is wrong both are at fault. What slaves we are to the boss, usually rightly. He is there—presumably—for his talent in being right. I remember one day in around 1955 taking a cricket side down to open the new ground at Scunthorpe. This was going to be a good day for me because the yardmaster, Bill Nock was going to bowl the first over and I was to receive it. Bill was well stricken in years and I was looking for some easy runs. And so it proved. However, before we got to Scunthorpe we came to a long halt at Stainforth. There was a derailment ahead and an Inspector was doing his stuff with single line working. After a look up in the signalbox I settled in the brake to talk to the guard, Merrydown.

'Dost tha know Charlie Bird?' he said. I drew myself up to my full height.

'I know Mr. Charles Bird our General Manager, yes'. Repressively.

'Ay, that's Charlie. I were at school with Charlie. Brightest lad in 't class; sat in 't middle of class did Charlie and when Charlie went wrong we all went wrong'.

I kept that story untold until C. K. Bird had his presentation on retirement. Alas, he died first. The moral for all of us who become Chairmen is to be Charlies but not proper Charlies. We mustn't go wrong.

Somewhere along this road I remarried. After Norrie died, brother Michael and wife Jacquie, living at Wadhurst, middle-aged, childless, said 'Come and live near us and Jacquie will be a mother to your orphan flock'. So I bought a small box of a house near Mayfield and settled down with Bron (17), she doing a secretarial course at Tunbridge Wells. We promptly found ourselves in the lurch because, with the inevitability of farce which dominates my life, Bro' and Jacquie started a family of their own and hardly came near us. They had two boys quick.

The neighbours rallied round, Hilda Hawkins next door and Diana Shervington, wife of Rupert of the Southern, in particular. And Joslin at Cambridge, Michael at Winchester and Ivor at prep' school got some basic training in the holidays. Luckily, I was not away from the office or from home often. 'I will give them all to the nation and no one shall ever look upon their faces again' is a fair description of life in 222 Marylebone Road.

Then Jo took her finals and got a Class II:I. This was pretty good for her since her extra-mural activities were constant and hectic. Jean wrote congratulating her. Jean had been the kid sister in the house where Norrie had lived when I was training at Parkeston in 1931. She had eventually grown up, married and had two girls, Inga (for mother was Norwegian) and Margaret. Her marriage had gone wrong during the war and since then she had looked after mother till she died, sometimes being cashier in a bank and sometimes the power behind Cockerell's the restorers of ancient manuscripts and books. Norrie and she had always kept in touch.

Joslin came down from Cambridge, did six months translating for Shell, then time for Punch. One day she announced she was going to New York to become the lure in the shop front of Tiffanys on Fifth Avenue. She wrote that I was to meet her in the Festival Gardens half an hour before her train because she had something serious to say.

'D', she said, 'you must marry again'.

'Who would have a fat, bald, ugly, old man like me?'

'Lots of people'.

'Well, who?'

'Jean Val, for instance'. When Jo came back from New York six months later, very brittle and gay, living on oranges and black coffee, I said:

'I'm taking your advice'.

'What about?'

'Marrying Jean Val'.

She burst into floods of tears. Women!

Therefore, if this is a sufficient chain of cause and effect, presently and after the proper preliminaries, Jean and I married. We bought a ramshackle Tudor farmhouse at Radnage in Buckinghamshire and set about the task of integrating our families. It took a long time. Jean has had a lot to do with my conversion from an introvert.

The other principal activity in planning and development was that on Liner Trains. I don't know who thought of them. Certainly Ralph Wilson aforesaid was talking at Liverpool Street on those lines in the early 1950s. Certainly piggy-back and Flexivans and so on in the United States have something in common. Nevertheless the idea of a national network of trains in fixed formation carrying nothing but containers for transit between any two customers in the land was something that neither existed nor was projected on any railway in the world. Certainly also it was not I who thought of it. My orders to set up and control a team to develop the project came from Freddie Margetts. As with every one of Fred's activities there was enormous drive behind it and an enormous personal contribution from him.

We got to lead the team Peter Keen. Peter had been Personal Assistant to Sir John Elliott at London Transport and as with all of them was being groomed for stardom; rightly; he has a first class brain, imagination and great charm of manner. Bill Johnson picked him out and sent him to me at Great Northern House. I promptly and rightly got rid of him into the Division for some rough-and-tumble training in basic railways. Somewhere along the line he married Paddy the daughter of our Deputy Chief Controller at Cambridge; which was certainly relevant to basic training. Peter got hold of Philip Satchwell from Costing and Michael Connolly from Operational Research. Hampered by Freddie Margetts, John Ratter, Philip Shirley, Hugh Barker and myself, for none of us could resist stirring the pot, they produced a scheme and costings of high promise. Between main centres for distances over 300 miles Liner Trains are a clear winner; between 200 and 300 they have a significant advantage; below 150 miles road will continue to predominate.

Therefore the really good routes would be between Scotland and England south of the Trent; the routes on which we would have a significant advantage would be between Scotland on the one hand and Lancashire, the West Riding, Nottinghamshire on the other; between London on the one hand and Lancashire, the West Riding, Teesside and Tyneside on the other; between South Wales, London–Birmingham, Sheffield–South Wales and so on. A lot of business; at the first count around sixty million tons a year.

Let us be clear on what grounds we were going to compete with road: on cost alone. Except for distances upward of 300 miles—and in the U.K. the land hauls over that distance are very few—road transport gives an entirely satisfactory service in safety, speed, reliability and convenience. Between say, 7 p.m. and 7 a.m. a lorry will run 250 miles with a load under constant supervision with ready communication with customer or employer, if anything goes wrong on the journey. Let us railwaymen not think we can do much about safety, speed, reliability and convenience except to pull out the beam from our own eye.

On cost we can have an advantage. We have the pay load of some 500 tons transferred between road and rail by some six men. We have the steel wheel on the steel rail. In spite of the extra two handlings the other two advantages added up to an advantage over road of some 30 per cent in cost. It was enough. Dr. Beeching and Margetts wrote it into the Report on the Reshaping of British

Railways published in the spring of 1963, debated and approved by Parliament in the summer. Merry-go-Round and Liner Trains were to be the two pillars positive and not negative, on which the future of British Railways was to depend.

The methods and prophesies which Peter Keen and his team enunciated are proving correct. On the first routes freedom from damage, reliability, speed and cost have been very much as the first studies predicted. Competitively, Scotland to south of the Trent has been a runner without argument. Tartan Arrow, Tayforth, Transport Development, B.R.S. have jumped on the bandwagon. At distances around 200 miles—and curiously very many of our principal centres of production and consumption lie just about that distance from one another—the battle is joined.

The story of Liner Trains is one of first class planning and development. Alas, it went beyond that. I have written earlier that my idea of a backroom officer's job at Headquarters was to get new ideas and to develop them only to the point of proving their feasibility; then to hand them over to the Regions to implement and myself to go on to the next idea. The Great and Good Doctor said to me one day talking at large about someone coming new on to the Board: 'The most difficult transition in industry is from management to direction'. The lesson has not been learned. Routes, rates, equipment, sales; there is at the time of writing through the fault of no one except the direction at 222, Marylebone Road, gross delay and exaggerated cost in getting schemes off the ground. Recently a Regional Planning Officer told me that someone at 222 had opined that at the Liner Train terminal at Stratford we should require a third reception siding. 'This will' he said without surprise 'mean redrawing the whole plan. The next plan will be the twenty-first we have drawn.' Charlie or proper Charlie I threw a veto at him. Next I demanded a meeting at 222 about Liner Trains. I got it and, bless them, heavy support from the planners and engineers for the proposition that by now we should have made up our little minds about principles and left it to the Regions to apply them. But from the Commercial side 'The revolution in transport is so fast that plans must constantly change'. I reflected on a meeting only a fortnight earlier at which the Commercial representative had arrived under instructions to press for a change from 30 feet containers to 20 feet containers in our new ships for Parkeston Quay. At the same meeting was the naval architect with the drawings of the ships based on 30 foot containers reporting that the contract to build them had been let. At this point I refrain with regret from a lecture on first principles of management.

I do, nevertheless, ask the question how many new ideas like merry-go-round and Liner Trains have been lost or delayed because the Central Direction has been trying to manage instead of giving itself time to think. May be it should instal a bath.

Another principal activity was the structure of the inter-city passenger service. It was ten years since Stuart Ward and I had evolved the philosophy of speed and frequency which would keep railways competitive with road and air. It was eight years since I had expounded that philosophy to the Railway Students' Association. It was two years since I began to sap and mine in the Corridors of Power to make internal services at end to end speeds of 70 to 75 m.p.h., the policy of the British Railways Board. Now with the support at Traffic Conference of Robert Long, Harold Few, Derek Barrie and Harold Hoyle, a minute was passed and was subsequently endorsed by the General Managers and the Board.

The next task was to translate it into timetables, which was none of my business. It is rightly a Regional responsibility to design and manage its own timetable in accordance with principles laid down by the Board: and I was no person, whatever the temptations, to abrogate my own principles in this matter. Nevertheless, if there was a deficiency in equipment it was my job to write the broad specification to remedy it. And there was such a deficiency.

The arithmetic in 1951 had shown that for end-to-end averages of 75 m.p.h. for the non-stop business expresses and 70 m.p.h. for the rest we would require over 3,000 h.p. under the bonnet. We should, if we were sensible, add about 15 per cent to give some headroom so as not to blast along at full throttle all day. We should add another 300 h.p. to diesels for taking eventually electric heating off the main generator. The net requirement for electric traction was 3,450 h.p.; for diesel electric 3,750 h.p.

Electric traction was easy. The designs for the London Midland's electrification gave that power—indeed more, because short periods on electric can grab out of the wire virtually unlimited energy. So I left Chief Electrical Engineer Stanley Warder alone. He had already done his stuff. I trotted off to Chief Mechanical Engineer, J. F. Harrison, and said: 'Four thousand horsepower, please'. Freddie has when shocked a disarming habit of leaning forward on his desk for a full half minute then slowly relaxing back in his chair and saying mildly 'What?' I repeated it. He searched for words for a long time then he said: 'Look, Gerry, I am up to my ears in this bloody diesel lark. The most we have got now is 2,500. Sulzers are coming along with 2,750 and that's your lot'.

'What's wrong with the Deltics?' A bad move this.

'Everything. High-speed engines are no good. They won't last—you'll see. Why not double head?'

Freddie always had a Thing about the Deltics. He could shut his eyes to the fact that they were 25 per cent more powerful than any other locomotive, that they were running double the mileage of any other and that their availability was the best in the country. I have always had a Thing about double heading. It stemmed from being a Gresleyite and therefore in favour of the big-engine policy and against the Midland's habit of hanging a second engine on the front passim. In any event the prospect of having on the now prevailing turn-rounds at King's Cross two 70 foot locomotives bringing the train in, two taking it out, triplet dining car, three brake vans and seating for about 40 passengers, all this daunted me.

However, I kept at him and was beginning to make a dent in the defences, when firstly I left and secondly the Sulzer 2,750 h.p. engine developed serious faults of design and distracted all the 'rude mechanicals' from trying yet another New Thing. The 4,000 h.p. locomotive is just beginning to come over the hill now, more than three years after the Traffic Conference Minute and over 12 years after the basic thinking which made it or electrification inevitable.

Apart from new ideas and their development the third leg of the task was to act as a spur and a stimulus to performance. Current operating performance is measured by safety, punctuality, convenience, comfort, economy. I did not judge that it was any part of my job to be hounding the Regions for detailed explanations of poor performance—nor did I expect to be hounded myself by the Chairman or Members. Indeed I think the Doctor was rightly and sublimely unconscious of day-to-day operating work. Therefore the point d'appui was the results in general.

As a means of communication we had the Operating Committee. I was in the Chair with Harold Hoyle as Deputy, then:—

| | |
|---|---|
| for the London Midland: | Sidney Gould; later Bobby Howes |
| for the Western: | Bill Lattimer |
| for Scotland: | Dick Jackson |
| for the Eastern: | Stuart Ward |
| for the Southern: | Rupert Shervington |
| for the North Eastern: | Frank Hick |

John Vipond had used this body very largely to vet and endorse the proceedings of sub-committees. I did my best to change it to a 'force de frappe'. They should think and communicate their thinking through the Operating Committee to the rest of the land. We wrote ourselves new terms of reference in that sense.

The first task was introspective. Were we in a position to judge our performance in safety and the rest? The old statistics, most of them, demanded historically by the Ministry of Transport seemed out of date. Freight train load, wagon miles or net ton miles per hour, and speed meant little if compared with previous years in the light of the change in traction. Any mug could show improvements. What we needed was firstly a good plan in the timetable measured by prospective load and speed and utilisation of locomotives and crews; secondly, a measure how far actual operation matched the plan. Instead of easy going annual improvements we began to set tough budgets by an absolute standard.

The second task was also introspective. Our rules which governed operating safety had been growing accident by accident and bit by bit for over a hundred years. The Ministry of Transport's Inspectors had been critical of the wording of the relevant rule in one or two recent reports. I took a look at them with a new eye and was horrified to find to what an extent the railwayman's habit of not blaming anyone was embodied in the Rule Book. The passive tense was everywhere 'such and such shall be done' not 'the guard shall' and the 'signalman shall ...' The Operating Committee agreed with this view: they thought rightly also that the people who had been writing the rules for the last 50 years were not the people to rewrite them. We sent for a retired but not retiring Chief Operating Superintendent, A. P. Hunter. He took as a guinea-pig single line working and divided it, Preamble—Duties of the Person arranging single line working—The Pilotman's Duties—The Signalman's Duties—Drivers' Duties and so on. No alibis there.

In tackling the administrative side of safety we were fearing no particular evil. Nevertheless one overtook us, mysterious, persistent, intractable. I have related in the past chapters two stories of high speeds by freight trains; one where I was in the brake from Pyewipe to Whitemoor, one about Bill Hoole running down the Talisman. If these were highlights, speeds of up to 70 m.p.h. were common on the East Coast route. The fish and meat trains from Aberdeen ran block-and-block with the night sleeping car expresses. The general run of express freight on the East Coast route and in East Anglia was booked at an average of 40 m.p.h. which required 55–60 m.p.h. over long stretches. Even lower down the scale I have known empty mineral wagons at 60 m.p.h. Masher May, for instance, on a Saturday, if March Town were playing at home, would run a truck train in front of an express and if you shunted him for it would play hell. We very rarely indeed got off the road on plain track.

Yet in 1962 there started a series of derailments on plain track which at the time of writing show little sign of abating. At the outset it was identifiable. On different Regions but on the same class of train we had a few derailments of Pallet Vans. There was no common factor in the loadings; some were loaded heavily, some moderately, some were empty. The reports from the Regions pinned the trouble on the design of the springs. Freddie Harrison grounded the whole Palvan fleet except the few which had a wheelbase longer than ten feet.

The derailments abated for only a few weeks. Then a short wheelbase banana van was derailed, then ordinary fitted vans. The reports began to show signs of uncertainty. The District Officers would write: well, the springs on the wagon were slightly unevenly loaded; there were some slight irregularities in the track; the driver may have braked or accelerated just at the critical moment. And so the wagon hopped off the road. In short they did not know what the hell. Luckily this sort of derailment constitutes no great danger to the train itself or to other trains. It was a common factor that the derailed wagon ran straight and true on the sleepers giving the chairs and the sleepers if concrete a costly treatment but until it reached a level crossing or a pair of points it did not derail adjacent wagons nor break up itself. When it struck something which gave it a real jar usually the coupling and vacuum pipe parted and both sections of the train automatically came to rest.

We consulted not only the 'rude mechanicals' but also the Technical Research Department for a prognosis and a solution. Dr. Sidney Jones came up very quickly with a statistical prognosis but said that a solution would take at least 18 months. Bond, Harrison and Jones predicted that the solution would be prolonged and costly. We would probably have to choose between re-springing the whole fleet of fitted vans or building new to a longer wheelbase. Sidney Jones went further. He said 'the cause is Diesel traction'. Since at that time a quarter of the derailments were behind steam I scoffed. I also pointed out that the line on which diesel traction was as far ahead as any other, the Great Northern, and on which the speeds were highest, was virtually free of derailments on plain track.

As so often with mechanical problems the responsibility for safety was back on the manager's plate. The Operating Committee reviewed the trends each month. It discussed the possible solutions. To ground the fleet of fitted vans would do maybe irreparable commercial damage. In any event the trouble had spread to other types, even modern types such as Presflo cement wagons and oil tanks. To specify minimum and/or maximum loadings would not help. The Western Region were getting heavily loaded wagons derailed, others lightly loaded or empty. To abandon diesel traction, ha ha? To reduce the speed of the express freight trains. Speed had not appeared as relevant in at least half of the cases. However not knowing what else we agreed that if any sharp increase took place we would reduce the maximum speed of all freight trains to 50 m.p.h. In April 1963 there were six derailments on plain track. For no reason other than that we judged the risk was now too high, we took on the telephone a decision to reduce all freight trains to a maximum speed of 50 m.p.h.

This had an immediate effect of reducing the derailments to about a quarter—one or two a month. This was to me an acceptable rate. People talk about the safety of railways as if it was an absolute thing. It is in fact very relative. I have indeed read or heard of no absolute standard of safety except in the historic and unprintable rhyme whose last stanza is:—

More recent researches than Darwin's
Have incontrovertibly shewn
That absolute safety at Oxford
Is enjoyed by the hedgehog alone.

The improvement was in fact a lull. In 1965, a year after I left, the problem returned with greater force still. Speed was brought down again, this time with no effect. The Great Northern was still immune. Why? The Great Eastern this time has virtually no incidence. Why? This is all right for me now on the Eastern Region. But I would not accept the present rate. It is several times the rate which in April 1965 I thought too high. With no technical help to speak of in forming a judgment, decisions about safety are intensely personal. Nevertheless at whatever the odds, even a hundred millions to one, it may be the first combination of circumstances which causes an express to run into a derailed freight train. The odds however build up comfortingly quickly. A Member of Parliament wrote to Dr. Beeching once that each of his last 16 journeys on British Railways had been unpunctual. Our average rate to time was 83.5 per cent. I asked the statistical boys for the odds—23,000,000 + to one against. A very unlucky man. He should never, as James Flynn and I were later to suggest we did, take the Western Region deficit to Newbury and put it on a horse.

# Speed up

## CUTTING
## TRAVEL
## TIME

between

London (Paddington) and
Birmingham, Wolverhampton,
Shrewsbury, Chester & Birkenhead

From 10ᵗʰ September 1962

New 2,700 H.P.
Diesel locomotives
More power
more speed

# 8

# GENERAL MANAGER, PADDINGTON

In the Autumn of 1963 our affairs were not prospering. Jean had had an operation at short notice and it had turned out a major affair instead of the minor one forecast. We had been backwards and forwards for treatment and were keeping our fingers crossed. At 222 Merry-go-round was hung up to dry. The Central Electricity Generating Board had accepted the system for all new and some existing coalfired power stations, but at the other end my Lords Beeching and Robens had got into deep sand about who should pay for the rapid loading equipment at the collieries. Liner Trains were in the inevitable second stage where after the initial impetus the rats of doubt were gnawing at the edges. The Wagon Authority had been formed—and, rightly formed—under Harold Hoyle but had taken an interest of mine away. The replanning of freight movement in order to close the Great Central Main Line and one of the Trans-Pennine routes was beginning to run into a political mess.

This is where and why no management should ever try to turn a 'Doer' into an Adviser. He has neither patience nor skill at being the Hidden Persuader. Rather he runs round banging on doors and shouting insults at the people inside them. Freddie Margetts did his best; 'Take an interest in the branch line closure programme' he said. 'I am Chief Operating Officer', I snapped back 'I can't operate No Service'.

As so often rescue was round the corner. I relate the next two incidents because I believe them to be related; no one else has or will. Earlier in the year the Golfing Society had asked me to be Captain, because they were in trouble about getting teams. People were taking notice of hostilities by the Vice-Chairman about the virtue of hard work and the indignity of golf in B.R.B.'s time. Spiking that sort of gun is easy. I took on the captaincy and got the Chairman to be President. What I had forgotten was that when he played he and I would play the top match together. So one day in September the Good Doctor and I with our unsteady 18's went forth to do battle with Troughton (7) and Elwes (13). When against all probability we strode back through the crowd round the last green, triumphant by 4 and 3, Freddie Mills our secretary, said in a loud aside 'Well that was one match I knew we would lose!'

Next week I took Jean off to Blakeney for a few days to stay with Canon Alan and Sadie Gates. On Monday the phone rang.

The Chairman: 'Can you get up tomorrow?'

I demurred but as always with him, vainly.

He was going on holiday and it wouldn't wait till he got back, so we set off: I dropped Jean at home and presented myself.

'Gerry', he said, 'there are going to be some changes. Raymond and Ness are coming to the Board. You are going as Chairman and General Manager at Paddington'.

There was a silence, stunned on my part.

Then 'I think', I said, 'that is taking me out of my class'.

There was the small hooding of the eyes and the twitch of the lips which means he is on a winner.

'I don't think so', he said very slowly, 'provided you keep your mouth shut'.

So I went back to Doing, and no moaning at the bar. On October 3rd I was in the seat once held by Felix Pole, James Milne, Keith Grand, Roy Hammond and Raymond. Raymond's Deputy, Lance Ibbotson had also gone to Marylebone Road; indeed I had asked that he should. He and I would have been incompatible at Paddington. We are two of a kind; hard-bitten Operators; there is no point in having two like that, one over one.

Raymond took great pains with the hand-over. He had opposed my appointment on the ground that I was too amiable—a judgment which he has kindly reversed since. Nevertheless he spent a lot of time with me over shopping lists of things in hand, plans for the future, organisation, thumbnail sketches of people. It was a great tour de force. Then the open hand clenched and he hit the desk a crashing blow. 'Remember' he said 'I love this place. I love the people. I don't want to go. I shall keep a hand on it. I shall be General Manager here as often as I want to be'. I said amiably 'All right, Ray' predicting correctly that he would involve himself so quickly and so deeply in his next job that he wouldn't have time to boss me around.

Paddington was in a curious mood. Till Raymond went there, they had successfully resisted infiltration from other Regions. Ibbotson had been almost the only newcomer. Raymond had come to shake them by the neck. 'I have had to keep sticking pins in myself to be beastly to you' he told their Debating Society, when he left after his 19 months. He had gone like a destroying wind through the traditional practices of the Great Western. He had symbolically stripped the works of Brunei and Pole and Milne from the Board Room and the corridors down to the basements and cast the attitudes to the four winds. The staff were at odds about it all. Many were frankly bolshie; many were dazed; some were frightened; some were in transition from those three states of mind to the knowledge that something very useful had happened to them; very few were wholeheartedly on Raymond's side.

He had made a most impressive start. He had just about halved the Region's deficit of over £30m. He had reformed the financial administration so that he got figures of revenue and expenditure within days of the performance. He had set up financial control of investment from the birth of the idea to the day of completion. He had torn up and sold redundant assets worth millions; cut stores, debtors and working capital. He had bullied the Western from last but one in the queue for diesels to the front position. He had cut at the root of some amiable policies about cheap fares, rates and charges. He had swung at the staff establishment with a devastating axe.

Nevertheless there was still a deficit of £15m. I have a simple philosophy about losses on railways. A railway which serves large cities lying between 50 and 300 miles apart; which has a coalfield; which has a large steel industry; which has no more than an average proportion of green fields; such a railway has no business to make a loss. If it does, then no one and no thing but the management is at fault.

It was also true that in spite of the Great Western's reputation for speed and punctuality—both phoney—the express passenger service was slow and unreliable; the suburban service extravagant; and the freight service could do with an overhaul.

It seemed to me that without the vast capacity of Raymond for do-it-myself, my line must be a display of amiability and a policy of setting competent people free to do things for themselves. We had a highly competent and in some respects brilliant top management—James Flynn (Finance), Bill Lattimer (Operating), Tommy Matthewson-Dick (Engineering), Sidney Ward (Staff), Bob Hilton (Cardiff), Dudley Hart (Bristol), Paddy Phillips (London), and David Pattisson (Plymouth); soon reinforced by James McBeath (Commercial).

The display of amiability was easy. I went immediately on the Great Western Railway (London) Golfing Society's annual weekend at Burford. I played lousy golf. They laughed themselves sick. They took my money off me at poker, and movies of me from my most obtuse angle—behind. They showed these to their Annual General Meeting and laughed a lot more. This was good for amiability but bad for discipline. So the next year I had had five lessons. I won the Medal starting with two birdies and a par; James McBeath and I won the Milne Trophy: I was second in the Greensome which entitles you to a reward known as The Captain's Balls. And I have been reminding them ever since that management like golf is only a matter of application. There are no alibis in management or in golf.

Secondly I called a meeting of the Chairmen and Secretaries of the Sectional Councils so that they could have a look at the new Old Man. I told them for 20 minutes how I thought a railway should behave; and they told me for 40 why it shouldn't behave like that at all. It came back to me afterwards 'Same as Teazy-Weazy Raymond but with kid gloves on'. Nearly right.

In passing poor Ray could no more avoid association with hair-dresser Teazy-Weazy than H. C. Johnson with band leader Snakehips.

As soon as they were open we adjourned to the Norfolk and got pints in our hands. Jan Evans of the Enginemen's Council came up to me.

'General Manager' he said in the lovely lilt that Norrie had so adorably when she was excited, 'do you know the Steel Company of Wales?'

'Yes'.

'Ah, but do you know the Chairman Sir Julian Pode?' A very elongated Po-o-o-de.

'No, but I am meeting him at lunch soon'.

'Ah, beware of him, General Manager, he is a very crafty man'.

Good as gold. Warning the new boy of supposed danger to our undertaking which he foresaw. It was from that moment that while I was at Paddington I was Western over the ears.

Thirdly, I had a bit of luck. In the first weeks I ground my teeth a good deal about the 'Loco' performance. The diesels were new and the drivers were chary of running at full throttle. 'Notch-four men: not top-notch men' I used to tell Bill Thorley. One day James Flynn and I were on the way to Cardiff; we were working. As we went through Swindon the rush and clatter seemed impressive. I looked at my watch. We were nine minutes early! At Newport I said to James 'I'll get on the footplate to Cardiff and tell the driver what a good guy he is'. So I climbed on, just flashed an engine pass at him and we set off. When we got past the not very easy colour light at the outlet from the tunnel, he relaxed and turned to me.

'They tell me the new General Manager's in the train'.

'Well he was but he got out at Newport'.

'DiO-O-O. He should have gone on to Cardiff. I wonder where the silly bugger's got to?'

'Here'. And he being Welsh, and I having had the mickey taken out of me when I thought to be taking it out of him, we both collapsed with laughter. This tale got round like lightning. Amiability was established.

As always before taking up a new job I had done some homework. It is worth quoting some of the vital statistics for the Western, remembering that they are adjusted for the transfer of territory to the L.M. (Banbury and North) and from the Southern (Dorset, Devon and Cornwall).

|              | 1955   | 1961   | 1963   | 1965   |
|--------------|--------|--------|--------|--------|
| Route Miles  | 3,700  | 3,500  | 3,115  | 3,000  |
| Stations     | 1,296  | 1,045  | 786    | 422    |
| Goods Depots | 1,100  | 989    | 775    | 231    |
| Locomotives  | N.R.   | 3,247  | 2,040  | 721    |
| Carriages    | N.R.   | N.R.   | 3,327  | 2,604  |
| Staff        | 92,380 | 75,000 | 62,435 | 48,252 |

The speed of the daytime express service with some comparisons was:—

|                      | Best | | | Average | | |
|----------------------|------|------|------|------|------|------|
|                      | 1939 | 1963 | 1966 | 1939 | 1963 | 1966 |
| **Paddington to:**   |      |      |      |      |      |      |
| Bristol              | 67.6 | 61.7 | 67.6 | 54.6 | 51.1 | 54.6 |
| Cardiff              | 54.1 | 64.5 | 67.0 | 50.3 | 56.2 | 58.5 |
| Plymouth             | 55.2 | 53.1 | 57.6 | 46.5 | 48.3 | 52.7 |
| Worcester            | 55.6 | 46.0 | 53.5 | 46.0 | 44.1 | 51.6 |
| Gloucester           | 54.8 | 57.1 | 56.0 | 44.1 | 47.0 | 48.2 |
| Wolverhampton        | 50.9 | 55.1 | 52.7 | 48.9 | 49.2 | 48.2 |
| **Liverpool Street to:** |  |      |      |      |      |      |
| Norwich              | 53.1 | 57.5 | 57.5 | 45.1 | 51.1 | 51.1 |
| **King's Cross to:** |      |      |      |      |      |      |
| Leeds                | 68.4 | 61.9 | 69.6 | 54.6 | 52.5 | 56.8 |
| Newcastle            | 68.7 | 67.1 | 69.1 | 55.3 | 58.0 | 61.9 |
| **Euston to:**       |      |      |      |      |      |      |
| Manchester           | 58.1 | 52.7 | 73.1 | 51.8 | 46.6 | 68.7 |
| **St Pancras to:**   |      |      |      |      |      |      |
| Manchester           | 53.0 | 59.9 | 48.8 | 50.0 | 49.5 | 47.5 |

With the Bristolian, the Cheltenham Flyer and the like the Western had established a reputation for speed which was enviable but phoney. The average speed of the service except to Bristol was poor. In 1953 when Stuart Ward and I were doing over the Norwich service, I had done my sums about speed and established that for effective competition with road over 70 miles and with air up to 300 miles we must have an average speed of 75 miles an hour, give or take a little according to the route. Even the business trains on the Western were many miles an hour short of this target. In spite of the slow speeds punctuality was rotten.

With the homework also a resolve: offer no criticisms; only recognise opportunities. It was good luck combined with Raymond that the diesels were coming along: and the planning of the timetable for higher speeds was not keeping pace. Like new Generals, new managers need an initial success. Knowing I was on a winner I started to preach punctuality coupled with not too overt references to the glories of the Great Western.

All that we really needed was to convert the notch four men to top notch men. So, Headquarters and Divisions, we all rode on footplates a lot; fleets of Inspectors were out. We featured punctuality in meetings, bulletins, at Sectional Council meetings. As soon as the drivers realised how much time they had in hand and that the nuts and bolts wouldn't work loose, we went to the top of British Railways punctuality League like a rocket. Now, this would have proved to be a great mystery to the British Railways Board if it had not been for one thing. They had just sent a new General Manager to Paddington—an ex-operator. He must be good. Such is the art of the charlatan. It was taking candy from the kids.

The culmination and final jape in the sequence came in the early autumn. Each General Manager had to report personally to the Management Committee on the state of punctuality in the

Region. The Management Committee consists of Board Members and General Managers. Bill Johnson and David McKenna had had a moderately rough passage earlier in the year. When my turn came I strode in, recounted our rise to the top of the first division, the all-time records broken; and, more shame to me, lectured them on how to do likewise; namely by hard work and of course expertise. They heard me in silence. Dr. Beeching asked for comment or question. More complete, utter, prolonged silence. I was on top of the world. I had in my pocket the next month's results which were markedly worse.

To be fair, while I had pulled the legs of the Board I had not done so with the staff. Earlier in the year when we had for the first time gone to the top of the League I had given a dinner at the Aldwych Brasserie to a selection of managers, inspectors, drivers, fitters, guards, shunters, examiners and had lectured them a good deal about how phoney we all were and how much work we all had to do. I had followed this up with a bulletin to the Region congratulating them but warning them that it could be a flash in the pan. It might not survive the acceleration of the timetable. I wrote about sloppy station work, bad regulation, too many not too good engines and not too good drivers. The last brought a counterblast from Driver Trevor Curtis of Landore, a well-known hammer of management. He accused me of 'denigrating the profession of driver'. I asked him whether, if I called Judas Iscariot a not too good apostle I was denigrating the profession of apostle. No reply; but he was very nice to me later when I met him.

In the matter of hastening slowly with speed in the express timetable there were very good reasons; 200 of them and more coming every week; the bloody diesels: many of them with high speed engines, most of them with hydraulic transmission, all of them with axles.

It was in my first month when Tommy Dick walked in one morning. 'The Penzance parcels was derailed last night'. Yes, I knew.

'It was a broken axle'. I sat up.

'It looks like a fatigue fracture'. I thought at once of Nevile Shute's *No Highway*, a story of fatigue in aircraft and the problems of the managers how to keep the service going.

'A D1000 it was. That axle had run about 180,000 miles'. Our main express passenger fleet.

'Tommy, how many axles have we got that have run that mileage?'

'Around 200; and of course they're doing over 2,000 miles a week'.

'Do we ground them?' I said, thinking of the replacement of over 60 2,700 h.p. locomotives by 1,700 h.p. Hymeks and the shambles which it would make of the timetable.

'No' he said slowly 'this is one-off. We start to examine all of them. A slow job, about six engines each weekend. We have to lift to get at the bogie'.

I thanked goodness for Tommy's steadiness. He found no more for a fortnight. Then in the third weekend one. We took no action.

*

In the fourth weekend three and I panicked. We took them off expresses on to freight. As so often—as I have written before—rescue was round the corner. Tommy Dick had been scouring the world for equipment so that we could inspect axles in situ and quickly. He had found the right oscilloscope in Canada. He had three flown over. Next week the D1000s were back to 90 miles an hour.

We had to replace every axle: not only on the D1000s but also on the Hymek D1700. One weekend the oscilloscope at one depot, Laira, found seven axles flawed. We are at the time of writing going through the same lark with much of the Eastern Region's fleet. Why can't people design axles? George Stephenson could.

Unlike the East and West Coast routes the lines out of Paddington are not easy for really high speeds. Certainly as far as Wootton Bassett Brunei engineered a magnificent highway, flat, straight, solid. Then he plunged into the hills, up and down and round them. Later someone else laid the line to the west between Reading and Castle Cary as a thoroughly bad railway. It runs down the valley of the Kennett and through the Marlborough Gap. The valley is broad. The river winds from side to side. The railway turns sharply as often as the river because whoever engineered it, so it seems, refused to build a skew bridge. I said this to Driver Perfect of Old Oak Common one day after for the seventh time in 20 miles he had braked for a speed restriction. His eyes didn't leave the road ahead. He said laconically 'When they built it they got paid by the mile'.

The first step in speed was the Golden Hind. Raymond had set up a new Divisional Office in Plymouth under David Pattisson. This was at the time a good move. The West Country were pretty bolshie about railways, and with some reason. The Beeching Plan, approved by Parliament in 1963, intended nearly a clean sweep of the branch lines. The Main Line from Plymouth to Penzance was suspect. There had been some rumours that we wanted to get out of the port of Fowey and lose the half million tons of china clay which it shipped. A study into the competitive routes between Exeter and London, S.R. and W.R. had begun with the obvious implication that one would either be closed or relegated to local use. The bums were in.

David Pattisson is a shrewd operator. He set out to revive the West Country. Firstly he made a friend of one of the principal railway critics, a journalist and publisher, David St. John Thomas. Secondly he did one thing. Now when you declare an intention to a hostile audience, to do one thing is vital. Nobody believes you when you tell him things; one thing done and they are on your side and content. I have before now averted a strike over a delay in building a shunter's cabin by sending down a man with a spade to dig a hole. Everyone was happy. 'They've started. There's our cabin'. Weeks later—this was in a bad time—we got another contractor to replace the one who had packed the job in and really made a start. David did better than this, he gave the West Country a whole new train; the fastest ever run from Plymouth. Taunton to London, 143 miles in 123 minutes; six D1000 locomotives, 'the Golden Stud' specially maintained; no phoney axles; hand-picked stock; hand-picked crew for the dining car; all seats reserved; Publicity. Press trip. T.V. He didn't forget a connection from the Penzance line. He thought of and got the lot. Within a month the load factor both ways was over 50 per cent: in three months it was over 70 and going up. We were turning people away on five journeys a week.

The West Country said: 'Here is someone who wants to save our railways' all in capitals. Then they complained bitterly to me that he wouldn't allow cheap fares on the Golden Hind. One member of Parliament—and he was a Tory—was greatly affronted about my cavalier attitude to public service (a term which was not within my duty under the Tory 1962 Transport Act) when I replied that if we can fill the train at full fares why should we overcrowd it with cheap?

We then started on the general structure of the service. We had little road competition but some by air from Exeter and Plymouth—neither very serious, and a good job too in view of our physical difficulties. The big question was whether to run the service with London to Waterloo or Paddington: and if to Paddington whether via Westbury or via Bristol. We did our arithmetic. For Exeter itself there was little in it in time because although Westbury was more direct it was slow between Castle Cary and Reading. From beyond Exeter the advantages of Paddington were overriding because to go to Paddington avoids the reversal at Exeter St. Davids and the climb of 1 in 36 to Exeter Central for the 60 per cent of our traffic which was with places west of Exeter. Rupert Shervington the King Operator at Waterloo still grinds his teeth about the conclusion.

Two principal advantages flowed from the decision. We could fill every other train plus the Golden Hind and still run Taunton–Paddington non-stop. The West Country therefore got a fast service. Secondly although the line from Exeter to Salisbury must survive on the traffic which it generated itself, the disappearance of the West Country trains on a Saturday—this single fact—would enable such a simplification of track and signalling and staff that the line would pay its way.

At this moment, the great and good Doctor threw a spanner into the works causing a shower of sparks and ugly grinding noises. He had not many outward and visible signs of human frailty, but one sign was his love of maps and another his love of publishing them. There began to be rumours of another map: then that it was to be trunk routes: then it was to be black lines, grey lines and no lines. Presently Planning Member James Ness took off the wraps.

It was a great tour de force. He summoned the brass of the Centre and the Regions to a hall. There he said that four people had gone into cells to peer into the geographical future of the trunk network. Here were the four people; an economist, an operational researcher, a planner, and an operator; and here—flick,

flick, flick, flick on the screen—were the maps. The four maps, arrived at by such different people, were to all intents and purposes the same. They must be right. It was, I imagine, like the production of the Authorised version of the Bible; 20 monks in 20 cells, identical wording. It was far better stage managed by James Ness.

Back in the office, I sat forlornly in front of my authorised version. No railway west of Plymouth. No Exeter–Salisbury. No Taunton–Westbury–Reading. In a while I rallied. I said to myself (I have a shocking habit of communing silently with myself in words) 'Look chum; you got a personal reproof from the Minister for saying publicly that the principal effect of the 1962 Act will be to make another Transport Act a certainty. Likewise, this map ensures the next. A lot of it is nonsense. The person who wants something is stronger than the person who doesn't want him to have it. Do you want these railways? So ...'

There was one thing wrong with that philosophy. I wanted the railways and eventually got them. The Doctor wanted publication: and he got it. In the teeth of the General Managers and a majority of the Board he published it. The scythes and pitchforks came out all over the West Country. The march on Paddington had begun.

I had at least saved a little. West of Plymouth; Exeter–Salisbury; Taunton–Westbury–Reading were in as grey 'routes not for development'. Naturally it was with some suspicion but not overt hostility that M.P.s began to arrive. Cornwall—James Scott-Hopkins, Greville Howard, Geoffrey Wilson, Dame Joan Vickers, Ian Fraser, Sir Douglas Marshall (later Peter Bessell). Devon—Jeremy Thorpe, Robin Maxwell Hyslop, Sir Harry Studholme, and so on. Before long came deputations from Torbay and the localities. In passing, General Managers W.R., never call the line from Newton Abbot to Torbay 'the branch'. Luckily—see earlier—we had 'dug our hole'. David Pattisson had put on the Golden Hind.

Although we made no bones about our intentions to close most of the branches—and this was mostly Tory country with M.P.s who had voted Aye to the Beeching Plan—we had also a good story to tell: it was the second area, after East Anglia, in Britain to be dieselised: much capital expenditure on diesel depots, new station and offices at Plymouth, new signalling and long welded rail.

We flew kites about development; accelerations on the Westbury route just round the corner; plans for a car-carrying train; plans not to get out of but to modernise Fowey; plans to get from Coastwise Transport the china clay to Kent and the potteries; to canvass the coal for the power stations and Gas Works. In all some million tons of traffic a year. This all sounded like a plan for a permanent railway: and so it was.

There were two snags. Firstly the general reaction to a request for help in getting traffic to rail is for M.P.s or Councillors or leaders of deputations to draw themselves up to their full height and say: 'Help? Who? Me?' It is fun to be able to go gently to work: 'Yes, you. You and your Government made it my duty to break even taking one year with another without regard for public service. I am duty bound not to run an unremunerative railway. I, General Manager, therefore want to run this bit of railway only if it is remunerative. You seem to want it. What are you going to do about it?'

On the way we were nearly blown out of the water by a broadside from Vice Admiral Hughes-Hallett, a Parliamentary Secretary to the Minister of Transport. He roared: 'If this traffic does not go by Coastwise Transport, how shall we take the British Army off the beaches of Dunkirk?' And indeed in time the Ministry under Section 53 of the Transport Act 1962 ruled that we were competing unfairly with sea and instructed us to increase our rates. Our customers and friends were so angry that they left the traffic on rail at the higher prices. After a while the

Government changed and John Peyton, M.P. for Yeovil said to me quietly one day: 'Remember; The Admiral only fires blanks now'. Again we went ahead. The Clay Liner train to the Potteries, Gas Coal for Penzance, Electricity Coal for Portishead. The West Country was recognising that out of three forms of transport, road, sea, and rail, they could support only two and were choosing to preserve rail.

Dorset were in more uncomfortable shoes. We were concentrating the traffic with London from Exeter and beyond on the Westbury route. I made no bones about telling Dorset that the line between Exeter and Salisbury must survive on the traffic which it generated—in the main, passengers and milk. The price of survival was assent to the closure of the small stations, and to the pruning of the railway to a single line, simplified signalling and at stations to bare essentials of buildings and staff.

We urged on them the need to develop the county, emphasising that Wiltshire to the north and Hampshire to the south and east had made their railways secure. Dorset was a desert in between. As an earnest of good intent we put 'Warship' diesels on the expresses and multiple-units on the local services. We drew up timetables to introduce as soon as the small stations were closed accelerating the expresses by up to 20 minutes and giving the remaining stations an express to and from London every two hours. Dorset started to manoeuvre. Keep Yeovil Junction open as well as Crewkerne and Sherborne within three or four miles on either side. Templecombe must stay. There was some business with 'bus operators so that they could not take up their licences. Tisbury, of course. One M.P. came and told me with every circumstance of glee that he had pruned a plan for the expansion of the principal town in his constituency down from forty thousand to fourteen. I got fed up with them; and they have got what they deserved: an express service far slower than before: and to my belief uncompetitive with road. In the long run unless Dorset firstly develops and secondly co-operates to let the railway use its advantage in speed, it will lose its railway. And serve it right.

In the meantime, Bill Lattimer having become Assistant General Manager for operation we had secured in his place the red-headed ball of fire Henry Sanderson. With John Palette, the operator at Bristol, and Leslie Morgan in Wales they made a great team for tackling the acceleration with Bristol and South Wales. The best railway work has no story and no panache. When I see Liverpool Street strolling through the evening peak, I know all is well but when they are brisking about there is trouble. So in brief we jacked up the best speeds to Bristol and South Wales to averages of over 65 miles an hour and the averages to the high fifties. We held the air challenge. The extension of M.4 and the prospect of the Severn Bridge did not worry us. Both these services as well as that to the West Country were contributing over 150 per cent over their direct costs. Good railway work by any standards.

On the other hand I made a complete hogsnorton of a bull like rush at the suburban service—no one's fault but mine. A recent study in 1963 had shown it to be losing over half a million pounds a year. It was slow, not very punctual; too many trains called at too many stations. The old boy network operated to such a degree that the Fishguard boat train called at Challow to pick up commuters. At Reading one day I stood gnawing my nails at the leisurely transfer of branch passengers to our already late main line. 'Blow your whistle at them' I hissed at the Inspector. 'Sir, we do not blow whistles at people from Newbury'. The train used to wait for Peter Hope at Pangbourne and George Goyder at Goring. I yearned for Old Joe who used to be porter at Rayleigh many years ago. 'It's time to go, Charlie. Two buggers running down the hill. Right away'. Much of the business of the Thames Valley we carried in main line trains weighing around 400 tons.

I demanded a new timetable based on maximum non-stop runs, high utilisation of the diesel multiple units, increased frequency and also a publicity campaign whose motto should be Happy Commuters and more of them.

The Mills of God ground on. George Gibb, Chairman of British Road Services Federation said to me one day in the 8.10 from Didcot: 'I hear you're going to make this service pay'. 'Yes, George' I said earnestly, 'and there is only one way. Make the customers stand'. The four Financial Times-es in the four corners came slowly down. Eight eyes made sure they would recognise me again. The four Financial Times-es went up again. Not a word spoken. I didn't heed the warning. You mustn't jape with people west of Liverpool Street.

We brought in the new service; a potential saving of £200,000 a year. 'Live on a Western Commuteroute', 55 extra trains a week, faster timings. Sheets of flame broke out in all directions. The stop Iver had had for 50 years was different. Challow had to travel not in the Fishguard Boat Express but ..., Newbury had a diesel multiple unit in which 'We can neither read nor write nor sleep'. I rode in it one day and approaching Reading broke my silence. I pointed out to a woman who had been complaining to her companion about us that out of 13 people in our section eight were reading, two were asleep and one, myself, writing. She went straight through the roof with one athletic bound.

They formed an association to defend themselves from us. They stormed Paddington; their leader refused tea in their name; he refused to sit down till he had made a speech for 20 minutes; he would listen to nothing in reply. He told a friend of mine afterwards 'I was so sorry for the General Manager. He looked so white and tired'. I was; white with rage.

Nevertheless I had committed a great stupidity. I had not made certain that the diesel multiple units were fit for outer suburban work. We retreated rapidly to the tune of about half the saving. We scoured British Railways for better multiple units but without success. So we turned to other things. The outward and visible sign in the organisation was that David Pattisson who had come to London as Divisional Manager just before the debacle, took over the suburban service very firmly and regarded me afterwards with an obviously avuncular eye. Nevertheless we saved something from the wreck. We had an increase of about 15 per cent in traffic. We had saved around £100,000 a year. Best of all we had got the punctuality right.

It had been one of the obvious gaps in the organisation at Paddington, and indeed of other Regions, that we had no effective organisation at Headquarters for promoting passenger sales. Paddy Phillips was the obvious choice. Cyril Lott and he were primarily responsible for a great success story. On Raymond's shopping list when I took over was an injunction to get out of the Fishguard–Rosslare and Fishguard–Waterford shipping services. The first of these was administered by a semi-independent Fishguard Railway and Harbour Board on which Coras Iompair Eireann had three members. Dr. Tod Andrews among them. The services made heavy losses. Nevertheless if there is one thing I like more than another it is semi-independence if I cannot have it complete.

At the moment of inheritance at Paddington Cyril Lott came up with a scheme for cutting a hole in the side of our St. David, clearing one deck and tarting up the cattle creep at Fishguard. Lo and behold a roll on roll off car carrier. Cost £85,000 within the authority of the local Board.

Off I went to Dublin: saw the Minister of Transport, Erskine Childers. He was entirely sympathetic with a forward policy. He doubted whether the threat of competition from a firm called Southern Development would develop. This wink was good enough. I have never signed a works order with greater alacrity.

In four months the St. David and Fishguard were ready. Admittedly it was a small embarrassment that the Board of Trade had imposed during the work some requirements which increased the cost to over £100,000 and brought me within the reach of the British Railways Board's financial disciplines.

Norman Lovenbury, our Public Relations Officer, produced a first class advertising campaign. Paddy Phillips got the motoring organisations interested. Bob Hilton spread the gospel around Ireland. The thing was an immediate winner. The St. David loaded to capacity through most of the season. Much traffic rubbed off on the St. Andrew and the B and I's Innisfallen. The service as a whole stopped losing money and, after depreciation at current replacement costs, made a profit into six figures. I was badly bitten with the excitement of going to sea: and indeed thought it all pretty easy. So I started out to lay plans for the future. Clearly, the four ships now working were too many. B and I's Innisfallen to Cork, Western Region's Great Western to Waterford, Fishguard and Rosslare Railways and Harbour Board's St. David and St. Andrew to Rosslare. In all, these four ships did in Winter only seven round trips: in Summer about 14. Two ships instead of four should do the lot. One would rush to and fro between Fishguard and Rosslare as fast as it could. Two round trips a day would be easy—14 a week. The second ship would do two trips to Cork, two to Waterford, and reinforce Rosslare with six trips at the weekend.

The Irish in the persons of Erskine Childers, Tod Andrews and Frank Lemass were all for this development. Indeed they wanted to take a greater share in it. They were at the time negotiating with Coast Lines to buy B and I. My proposals fitted in neatly with their plans. They agreed to go ahead with modernising Rosslare. They would lay out a new customs terminal and large car park at Ballygeary. They would convert one line of the railway viaduct which connects Ballygeary with Rosslare quay to a road. They would construct a tunnel for cars to get on to the St. David, and eventually on to our new ships. Later when these works were complete, I attended the opening. I sat at lunch between two Bishops, Roman and Protestant; and the Minister in his speech called me a 'friend of the country'. It warmed the cockles of my heart.

Before this, however, things had begun to go badly wrong. Our proposal for new ships had gone astray. The B.R.B. at that time had a very persistent bee in their bonnet that the Southern and London Midland had too many ships. In this they may have been right. Therefore, either the 'Falaise' or the 'Lord Warden' or the 'Dover' or one of the 'Dukes' from Heysham should be converted for Fishguard. David McKenna and Bill Johnson dug in their heels: David because the gap at Dover would promptly be filled by Townsend Ferries or another competitor: Bill because at that time—he has changed his mind since—he saw dangers to Holyhead from an alliance between the C.I.E. and the Western Region in the south. From this moment the issue was clear. The B.R.B. had to make up their mind either to build new ships for Fishguard or to take ships from other unwilling Regions. They did neither for over two years.

The upshot has been that the C.I.E., impatient of waiting for the western alliance went into partnership with B. and I. Frank Lemass and Liam St. John Devlin started a new container ship from New Ross near Waterford, not to Fishguard but to Newport. They charitably offered Lance Ibbotson a share. We had surrendered the initiative; and what happened served us right. It was my own fault. In my days at Liverpool Street I would have bulldozed or circumvented the draggers of feet. The man who wants something is always stronger than the man who does not want him to have it—if he wants it enough. Evidently I had not wanted those new ships enough.

In the second year we started a car-carrier between London and Fishguard. I had had experience of the car-sleeper between King's Cross and Perth which Geoffrey Coaker had organised to success by attention to fine detail. We decided not to repeat that pattern. Fishguard was 220 miles from London only, compared with over 400. The customers were not likely to be in the Bentley class. We wanted an out and home working for the stock: down by night, back by day. Paddy Phillips went to work and came up with the proposition that we treated the car as a container: that we should charge around £20 for the car. Into it the driver could load, without extra charge, himself, his wife, his family, dog, cat, canary, his ox and his ass and all that was his. This is not so ridiculous as it sounds. On the Corran Ferry last year I saw a Land-Rover with a family on holiday; at the back on one side was the baby in a pram, on the other, a donkey. Included in the charge was the use of a second-class compartment for the family. If two, lie down; if three, one lie down and so on. We expected to break even if we sold half the train. In connection we booked the St. David to run two trips a day, seven days a week.

Paddy did his stuff with the Motoring Organisations. Norman Lovenbury did a press and publicity campaign with himself as the central figure. The pink leprechaun peering through a steering wheel was a speaking likeness of Norman. By the end of February we had sold over 70 per cent of the space.

This was a great surprise to me. Previous market research had led me to believe that publicity did little to help. In my days at Great Northern House—first faltering steps in commercial work—we had questioned the £62,000 a year we were spending on advertising excursions in the London evening papers. We had surveyed the passengers using the 'Master Cutler' three months after it started. On the 'Cutler' in spite of press, poster and mail, three-quarters of the passengers said 'a friend told me'. No friend

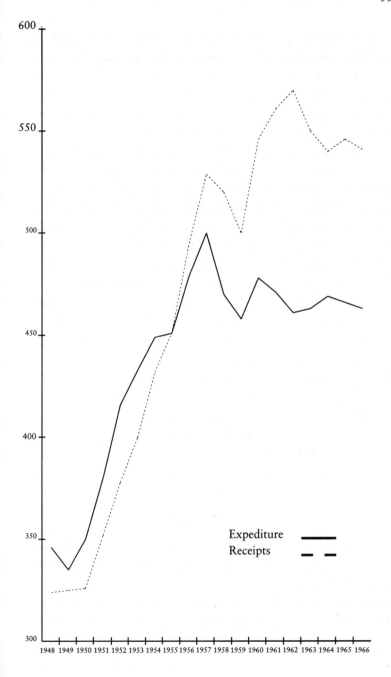

Expediture ——
Receipts — —

could tell another about the Fishguard car-carrier; it wouldn't start for another two months.

Paddy began to wonder what to do with the money. He added a buffet-car: and as the bookings outran the capacity, another carflat. Like Geoffrey Coaker for Perth, he spent a great deal of time getting the detail right: ease of pre-booking: simple documents: good direction to Olympia: pleasant attendance there: simple driving on and off. He ran trial trains before the day. He was ready in case the experiment of having no cover for the cars was a failure to instal an instant car-wash at Fishguard. The whole enterprise was a success. The car-carrier pleased everyone. It gave us a name for imagination and energy far wider than so simple a thing deserved. It made good money in its own right. It put the profit on the Fishguard service up to over £250,000 that year.

The remaining highlight at Paddington was the attack on the deficit. Things began to go wrong with the finances of British Railways in 1953, when the Transport Act of that year stimulated competition not only from the private sector of road haulage, but also from the public sector. From that time British Road Services were at us. The effect of this competition was that the revenue of British Railways did not continue to rise, as the expenditure continued to rise, *pari passu* with inflation. The revenue levelled off.

However we manoeuvred with passenger fares, schedules of freight rates, and individual bargains with our principal customers, we got no more money into the till.

By 1957 we were not even meeting our operating expenses. The operating ratio for that year (operating expense × 100, divided by revenue) was 105. Among the individual regions there was a wide disparity.

It is interesting to record the performance between 1957 and 1966:—

**Operating Ratio**

| Order | Region | 1957 | Worst point | 1966 | Order |
|---|---|---|---|---|---|
| 1. | North Eastern | 89 | 112 (1962) | 94 | 2 |
| 2. | London Midland | 100 | 136 (1963) | 131 | 6 |
| 3. | Eastern | 101 | 105 (1961) | 90 | 1 |
| 4. | Southern | 108 | 108 (1957) | 96 | 3 |
| 5. | Western | 124 | 138 (1961) | 108 | 4 |
| 6. | Scottish | 126 | 132 (1962) | 126 | 5 |

In 1966 three Regions had an operating surplus; one was on its way; and the principal losses on British Railways occurred in two Regions only. This is a powerful reinforcement of my earlier philosophy that a Region which has the potential stemming from an inter-city business, a coalfield and basic industry has no business to make a loss. In 1962 the ratio for this Region was 138. In 1963 with no enthusiasm at Paddington but grateful thanks from the Euston Confederacy, the Western's territory from Banbury to Birkenhead, including Birmingham and the Black Country with all of Central and North Wales was transferred to the London Midland; and with it went, as I calculated later on arrival at Paddington, a deficit of over £6m. a year. Indeed Bill Johnson now accounts for much of his unprofitable activities in terms of this dastardly deed.

The deficit at Paddington on the operating account in 1962 fell sharply to 129. Raymond had made them extremely conscious of finance. James Flynn had organised a first class system of financial reporting whereby on the morning of the fourth working day after the events we knew pretty accurately the revenue and expenditure for the previous week. This gave the Managers a prompt incentive to manage in financial terms.

As was to be expected, Raymond had achieved his successes in the fields of new works, and stores, and contraction. He had not—how could he have?—the beady London & North Eastern

Railway eye. It remained for me to attack in the operating and locomotive departments the tradition of the Great Western to employ three men where the L.N.E.R. would have employed two; to use two parallel railways where one would do, and so on. In other words it was jam for the bumped up timing clerk.

During the Staff Association's Conference at Newquay in May 1964, Jean and I had a day off. Our job was to be night hawks and keep the delegates full of beer after supper. So on the Monday we went off by train to Penzance. I walked up to the loco' depot. It was all gas and gaiters till I said to the Running Foreman:

'How many rostered turns a day?'

'Fifteen train working and two shed turning. The shed sets ferry an engine morning and evening to the station'.

'How many sets of men have you?'

'Thirty ...'

And so it was at Old Oak Common and many other places. When we got really going with Bill Lattimer, Henry Sanderson, Tommy Dick and Tony Parker, it became obvious that within a year or two we could carry with a staff of 40,000 the same traffic as had been carried a few years earlier with 92,000.

The rough accounts for the Region were going to go something like this:

|  | Income | Expenditure |
|---|---|---|
| Gross Revenue | £70m. |  |
| Salaries and Wages |  | £45m. |
| Materials, etc. |  | £15m. |
| Depreciation, etc. |  | £7m. |
| Expenditure |  | £67m. |
| Surplus | £3m. |  |

We were on our way. Every year since 1961 has recorded a significant improvement in the operating ratio. The annual average improvement has been six points—138 to 108 in five years. The Western ought therefore to break even within two years, a year later than I forecast to them. It is the greatest single disappointment in my life that I am not at Paddington to lead the greatest celebration of all time on the occasion when they restore the Great Western's tradition of earning an honest dividend.

# Modernisation...

# STAFFORD

## *New* STATION

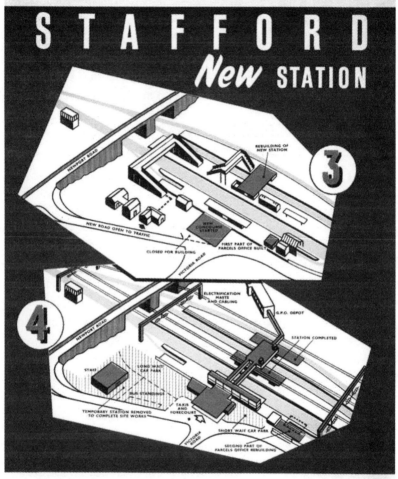

Besides the features of the reconstruction scheme already described, the new Stafford station will have a combined refreshment and waiting room where cooked snacks and grills will be served. There will be a lay-by directly off Station Road, for buses serving the town and surrounding places.

Another feature of the modernised station will be a direct bridge link between the G.P.O. Sorting Depot and the station which will avoid congestion by mail vans during peak hours.

Stage 3 of the modernisation which will be started in 1961 will see the completion of Newport Road Bridge. The new signal box will be brought into use, the new Station Road opened and the construction of the new buildings started on all platforms.

Stage 4 – the final stage. Work will commence on the concourse and booking office block and the new station will be completed and in full operation in 1962.

*BRITISH RAILWAYS MODERNISATION — Getting on with the job*

LONDON MIDLAND

# 9

## GENERAL MANAGER, LIVERPOOL STREET

In 1964 the Socialists narrowly won the Election. Good. We had voted Socialist; I for the second time in my life. The first time was in a local Election at Lambourne End in Essex in 1953. I was Chairman of the Conservative Association. The local branch while we were on holiday had selected as candidate a fast buck jumper half way through another planning fiddle and his fourth wife. Norrie went all galvanised. We decided to vote Socialist and let it be known. He got in by three votes; on a division, Norrie's and mine. Only the rector, and he out of charity, spoke to us for six months. Villages are hell.

In 1964 we thought that the Tories had had their chance for long enough to stop talking about getting disciplines into the economy and to act. The Socialists were saying, Me too. Let them try. So thought a lot of other people. They scraped in. We drew also a couple of other conclusions. Prices on the Stock Exchange would go for a burton; and sterling would be devalued. So let us sell our bits and pieces and buy a house.

Jean comes from Harwich. I too like the wide skies and the vigour of the great ploughlands of East Anglia. We set off to prospect the quadrilateral Southwold–Framlingham–Dedham–Frinton. In February we came to Aldeburgh. Small, ugly, no pattern about it; but a good wide main street, fishing boats on the beach, a lifeboat on its cradle, a mile to the station, two good golf courses, some people we knew. There were 36 points on our shopping list. Aldeburgh and the house we eventually bought fulfilled 33 of them. It was blowing a full gale on shore from the North-east. It was whipping the scud inland so that a mile ashore we tasted salt on our tongues. We tacked along Crag Path past the lifeboat. Jean said, 'This is where we want to live, isn't it'. No question mark. So in the fullness of time we bought Dartmouth just behind the lifeboat.

The next thread in the great web was a summons from the Chairman from Derby. It is an occupational hazard for me that whenever my boss wants me I am over a hundred miles away—and often glad of it. Anyway, I went on the next train. 'The Minister has approved your appointment as Chairman and General Manager of the Eastern Region. You will amalgamate it with the North Eastern and become Chairman and General Manager of both'. My nose for news has always been bad. I hadn't heard a whisper of this. Indeed, if I had heard I would have put a stop to it for several reasons. Paddington was fun. We hadn't balanced our books on which I had set my heart. Liverpool Street was a bit old hat for me. So much of what remained to do at Paddington had been done there. And, of course, it was another bloody reorganisation and this the most disagreeable of them all, namely the task of making redundant half of my lifetime's friends. However, the Minister had approved. No escape. The pressgang had got me.

Two or three times in my life I have been chosen to do a major reorganisation of an administration, Great Northern House and Eastern/North Eastern among them. This has always astonished me. I have never made a secret of my boredom by office administration. I have my fun in trains and Works and staff and public relations. Thank Goodness, I say, for Reuben Taylor at Cambridge; for that Napoleon of the Euston Road, A. V. Daniels at G.N. House; for Charles Whitworth at Liverpool Street, who see to it. Moreover, reorganisations are bad for trade. 'When you reorganise you bleed' said a visiting speaker at our Staff College at Woking. For many months the few top people who keep the momentum up are distracted from their proper job. Punctuality goes to hell. Safety starts to slip. Don't reorganise. Don't. Don't. Don't.

One corollary, of course is not to hire very top brass who know little about railways but a lot about organisation. They follow their bent, stirring the pot to its depths, distracting everyone, making everyone's head a bit loose on his shoulders for fear of the guillotine or Transportation, and railing all the while that punctuality and safety go down and the deficit goes up. And it serves them right.

So I marched off to Liverpool Street. We had a long interval selling our ramshackle Tudor farmhouse. We advertised it in the Times as 'full of character and worm'. In spite of this it was several months before we sold and moved to Aldeburgh, whence I commuted happily to London on the 7.18 Lowestoft. Two hours a day each way has given a powerful impetus to this book.

One consequence of the prospect of Aldeburgh was a personal involvement in the great row about the East Suffolk line. This is the opportunity for a general sermon about rural railways—not, I repeat not, unremunerative railways à la Beeching.

In 1962 the Marples/Beeching axis began to define their territorial ambitions about rural railways. They laid it down in general that rural railways did not pay, which was true; and could never pay, which was false. They did not, therefore, require more than the most elementary arithmetic on the losses either in general or in particular. They took no account of the new techniques; either coming into operation like diesel traction, or just round the corner like automatic level crossings, mechanised track maintenance, tokenless block signalling, and 'bus stop operation which can cut the cost of rural railways by more than half.

The upshot was that in 1963 the report on the Reshaping of British Railways, 'The Beeching Plan', was debated and approved by Parliament. Its positive side, Liner Trains, Merry-go-round, general productivity, are irrelevant here. What is most relevant is that one of the appendices to the report spelled out in fine detail the lines and stations from which passenger services should be withdrawn. Among these lines was the East Suffolk. The Eastern Region started to go through the drill—preparation of a case for the Transport Users' Consultative Committee; publication of intent; objections; hearing by the T.U.C.C.—report by them to the Minister—decision by the Minister—application for licences for alternative 'bus services; publication of date of withdrawal—withdrawal. It all takes a very long time. When I got to Liverpool Street in 1966 the hearing by the T.U.C.C. had just been held.

The lapse of time had enabled the Members of Parliament who had amiably and thoughtlessly trotted into the Aye lobby in support of the Beeching Plan and of the closure, among others, of the East Suffolk, to find out that they were holding a red hot electoral potato. The election in 1964 had left Labour with a scant majority. An election in late 1965 or early 1966 was a sure bet. The M.P.s turned tail.

When I looked at the situation I found ranged on the one side a serried phalanx of the M.P.s, the T.U.C.C, the local Press, the local populace, and the railway staff; on the other side the railway management. The latter were dashing at this phalanx with all the residual courage and waning enthusiasm of the last handful of

Kellerman's dragoons in front of Picton's squares at Waterloo. It was not enough. The battle was clearly lost.

The dilemma was whether to defend a last ditch or to withdraw in good order; and if to withdraw in good order, how? It was a misfortune that at Liverpool Street the planning people were thoroughly disciplined by B.R.B. policy. It was great good fortune that as Divisional Manager at Norwich we had Claude Hankins. He had been translated from Plymouth when we had abolished that Division in the previous autumn. I had caught up with him. He had done a lot of work in simplifying railways in Dorset and Devon and Cornwall.

We decided that the last ditch was untenable. The Minister would refuse to close the line. The railway management would appear as a malignant bureaucracy over whom a free people, through their M.P.s, had won a resounding and final victory. Anything which we did thereafter—if indeed we could do anything—would appear vindictive; an attempt to thwart the democratic will of the people, by a system of gradual strangulation and sabotage. These rash phrases are not mine. They are quotations from the local Press. The line would eventually die not from strangulation but from inertia.

Claude and I began to do our sums. The first one was that over 2,000 people a day used this line. We thought we could run a lot of railway profitably at that. The second was that the costs of the line had been represented to the T.U.C.C. at around £0.25m. For 45 miles this seemed enormous. We took the back of an envelope and started on the costs of a basic railway, 45 miles long.

Single line instead of double.

Automatic crossing loops.

Automatic or traffic light level crossings.

Unstaffed halts.

Conductor/guard operation.

Simplified fares.

High utilisation of D.M.T.U.s.

| The result was:— | £ |
|---|---|
| Maintenance and renewal of track. | 30,000 |
| Maintenance of signalling. | 2,000 |
| Crews, fuel, maintenance of 2 × 2 D.M.U.s. | 30,000 |
| –do– 1 hauled train. | 6,000 |
| Supervision. | 2,000 |
| Interest on £200,000 investment. | 14,000 |
| Total | 84,000 |

The revenue was around £120,000. We reckoned we might lose £30,000 by reducing and simplifying the fares. We would be in balance £90,000 to £84,000. As bonus we would have nearly £100,000 from the sale of the second track, buildings and land. With an eye on our duty—and pleasure—to break even financially, we laid our plans.

The principal plan must be how to induce this phalanx to break its ranks. We needed full co-operation from Councils and our own staff, particularly on level crossings, station buildings and bus-stop operation. After a ministerial refusal to close it would be easy for the phalanx to contrive to present an impregnable front. They could conveniently forget that under this threat of closure many of them had been urging British Railways to save the line by unstaffed halts, conductor/guards, automatic level crossings and the rest. We needed a gang.

Our first effort was a failure. On the recommendation of Sir Ian Jacob I approached the East Suffolk County Council to meet me. They refused. The matter was *sub-judice* with the Minister.

The next step we took should have been the first. We went out in full panoply of the Saloon on a tour of the line, meeting Press and T.V. In passing, it is fun, apart from being enormously useful commercially to have your own special train.

'Rail Chiefs bid to save East Suffolk' the Press began in February, and by slow and sensible editorial stages, got in July to 'Do it yourself rail travel has come to East Suffolk. The remedy may seem drastic but the choice was initially between closing the line and making the whole operating and maintenance staff redundant or running the line with a limited staff. The investigation ordered by Mr. Fiennes ought to have been started four years ago—that it came about at all is more a matter of self congratulation by the forces of public opinion ably interpreted by the Members of Parliament, supplemented by Mr. Donald Newby'. This stage took five months.

I asked Sir Edmund Bacon to give me a character with the County Council. This brought to Liverpool Street the Clerk, Lightfoot, heavily disguised, but when he tore off his whiskers, a very enlightened character. We had two hours. He dropped his spear, but remained ready to pick it up again if others did not break their ranks.

The next *point d'appui*—not of attack, because we were in full retreat—was the M.P.s'. We had two of them to lunch at Liverpool Street to let them see that we were human. Then we invited all four out on a tour of the line. They would be expected to make statements to the Press and on T.V. expressing solidarity with the railway management and approval of their plans. Life can get very difficult for M.P.'s can't it? Two of them during the last year or two had been thrashing the railway management for not adopting the very plans which we were now proposing. Yet now, if it were certain that the Minister would refuse the closure, there would be a political advantage in letting her take the blame for any diminution of facilities and for any redundancies. Two of them remained perched on the horns of this dilemma. Two, bless them, came straight on to our side. The phalanx had broken its ranks.

'There will be the hell of a row if after spending the day looking at this line and talking about these plans, we are told that it is going to close' commented one M.P. to the Press. 'These remedies were suggested five years ago and could have been put into operation then. It is symptomatic of what is wrong with Britain—that it has taken five years to decide on a plan which, with common sense, should have been done five years ago'.

Sir Harwood Harrison commented 'I am delighted by this new approach by the railways'.

By this time responsible opinion in East Anglia had changed its mind about three very important things; firstly, that Railway Managers do not 'run down services with the object of closing them' but rather enjoy running railways; secondly, that rural railways could not survive if they continued to be run at a very great loss; thirdly, that what we were doing to minimise losses or to convert a loss into a profit was sensible.

The change of front by the new Management had two further consequences, both embarrassing. The B.R.B. had its troubles in pressing the Beeching Plan on the Eastern Region under H. C. Johnson. Bill's attitude to closures was to say 'Yes, but isn't all of this a bit late, my masters? Taking off unremunerative services isn't a very new thing for the Eastern Region. We have only three stations open in the 80 miles between Peterborough and Doncaster. We closed 150 miles of railway when we did the Midland & Great Northern and so we know what we are doing. Go away and teach the Southern, and the Western, and the London Midland who haven't started'.

Then Bill went to the London Midland. Roy Hammond and Tim Bolland took over the Eastern; and the rule of law according to the Reshaping Report and of order according to the B.R.B. once again came to Liverpool Street and reigned for two years.

If there is one thing more comforting than another about law and order it is its massive and inexorable progress. In two years Roy and Tim had produced a lot of arithmetic, many reports in due form, and secured a number of hearings before the Transport Users' Consultative Committees, but had failed to bring the Minister to the point of decision. East Anglia, Lincolnshire, and South Yorkshire, were practically as I had left them six years before. With this salvation I was pleased. We needed some time to work out and apply the philosophy of the basic railway if, as expected, it halved the costs without damaging the revenue. In this respect Dr. Beeching's Reshaping Report was a dead letter. However, in the meantime we needed a holding operation in which Freddie Margetts and Roy Hammond, now at the B.R.B. and charged with the duty of carrying out the Beeching Plan were made to doubt the wisdom of a precise adherence to everything which was written. If anyone visited 222 Marylebone Road and daubed it with MENE MENE TEKEL UPHARSIN it was not I, but the message was clear. It put us all in an embarrassing position. Indeed, they wrote often and said so, not realising that this is one phrase which fails to stir the tender heart of a manager in the field, because it is his customary posture.

The other embarrassing consequence of the new Management was the rush to climb on the bandwagon. Eldon Griffiths, M.P. came up with a proposition to keep open Elmswell and Thurston, two stations under notice of closure by consent from the Minister. We agreed and indeed threw in Kennett and Dullingham for good measure. By doing so we retained receipts of some £8,000 a year. We avoided a bus subsidy of some £3,000 a year at a cost of heating, lighting and maintaining the four stations, and of fuel for stopping the trains of around £1,000. Of such is the crass folly of parts of the Beeching Plan.

One day a Mr. Douglas Brown wrote to me about the Stour Valley line from Marks Tey to Cambridge via Sudbury and Haverhill. We had just had from the Minister a refusal to close it between Marks Tey and Sudbury but a consent to close the rest. Mr. Douglas Brown had worked out a simplified timetable based on two diesel units running a shuttle service. It was a nice tidy effort, but the Stour Valley was not in the category of lines which we could make pay by conversion to a basic railway. So we took the second attitude 'This railway loses money. We see no prospect of making it pay. We have a consent to close most of it. If you want to keep it open, what are you going to do about it?' Douglas Brown went straight into the Press, crying to Heaven about my harsh and unreasonable attitude.

When I had told him twice more what I had said and that I had meant it, he organised a gang of the Local Council along the line to meet us and to negotiate how to keep the line open and what it would cost them to do so. At the time of writing the outcome is not certain, but the ploy had one effect. I found that in this matter I was much closer to the Minister's attitude than were the B.R.B.

The next stage in the public argument was the great storm in the teacup at Newmarket. Twenty years ago when I was Chief Controller at Cambridge, Newmarket had used the railway for trains of horses almost daily to race meetings all over the country, for trains to bloodstock sales; for travel by owners, trainers, jockeys, stableboys, to foreign meetings; for travel by foreign buyers to bloodstock sales, and by many hundreds of racegoers to race meetings at Newmarket. The local population travelled a great deal. The proportion of first class travel was high for a town of around 11,000; it contributed to the railway more per head of population than any other in the country. The railway blessed it accordingly with much managerial time ('knowledge of and interest in horse racing essential' never appeared in the advertisement for a District Superintendent at Cambridge, but was in at least Old Man Mauldin's mind at interviews); we blessed it with a handsome station. But when Claude Hankins and I arrived the traffic in horses had vanished to road and air. The racing fraternity by rail inward and outward had become a trickle. Newmarket was now a wayside station, contributing some 300 passengers a day, principally workers, schoolchildren and shoppers. When Claude proposed to treat it like the similar Saxmundham's and North Walsham's and convert it to an unstaffed halt, I saw no objection. When he went to Newmarket and told them they saw many. They ignored his offer to provide any facilities which they wanted at their cost. They started the usual political opposition. I came into it and so did the Chairman and the Minister. There were questions in the House. Since this was a matter for the railways to manage this tactic brought a brush-off from the Minister. The next effort was a smear campaign in the Press why a nationalised industry should waste public money building a glossy new booking office and issuing new uniforms to the staff if we were going to shut the one and sack the other. The answer to the first was that we were doing our best to revive travel but Newmarket had not responded. The answer to the second was that private enterprise was delivering uniforms up to a year late, and anyway we were not sacking the staff but transferring them elsewhere. Then they began to get nearer the mark with a deputation to Harold Few. He heard them but gave them no encouragement except again the offer of facilities at their cost.

The Press campaign started again; this time it took the line that they had no powers to contribute ratepayers' money for such purposes. It also reported that the Council were to seek an injunction to restrain us from unstaffing the station. General Sir Randle Feilden, the President of the Jockey Club came and had it out with me on the lines of the importance of Newmarket to the nation, the export trade and the bloodstock industry. I said 'But no longer, alas, is Newmarket station of importance to these things. Workmen, shoppers, schoolchildren—that is what Newmarket has left us with'. He didn't deny it. I offered him the station as Headquarters of the Jockey Club and let him go disconsolate. None of the horses would run.

The injunction, predictably, fell flat on its face. By this time it was December and the date of operation was January 1st. In Christmas week the Council sent a deputation to negotiate, asking for bygones to be bygones and for time to consider the matter. We let the names they had called us go—naturally, see what I have written about embarrassing postures. I refused more time. They had wasted four months in political manoeuvre, press campaigns, abortive injunctions. We requested next week a letter of intent to rent, and/or pay the cost of staffing the station, if they wanted those facilities. The Council met in a smother of mixed metaphors 'British Rail had a pistol in their backs', 'British Rail had them over a barrel'. If Claude had pulled the trigger, he would have caused a nasty flesh wound. And I confess that I enjoyed the notion that the Council would conduct its proceedings for some time standing up. We got our letter of intent.

In these ways we had made it clear in East Anglia firstly that where by altered methods of working we could see our way to making a rural railway profitable we were glad to keep it open; secondly that where there would be a continuing loss we were glad to negotiate with local authorities to keep a railway open or to provide facilities greater than we judged to be necessary, as long as they guaranteed the extra costs; thirdly that we were impressed only by reason and by direct negotiation with us. The effect of it all will be, I believe, to preserve a lot of railway which would otherwise have been closed and to avoid for many years a most costly programme of road works.

The rest of the passengers in the Eastern Region, inter-city and commuters, were in good heart. With what *The Economist* in an article on the L.M. electrification called 'mouldy old diesels' we were running on our main lines an express every hour between our principal cities, 'our' being defined to include the West Riding and Newcastle. We were at the head again of British Railways for punctuality. The track on the G.N. main line was magnificant. Both on the East Coast route and on the Colchester main line business was on the upgrade. In the autumn indeed B.K.S. withdrew their air service between Tees-side and London: and Sheffield did not proceed with a new airport scheme for this same reason.

The commuter services out of Liverpool Street were, except for the minor Lea Valley, fully electrified. Liverpool Street was running on three tracks 67 trains in the peak hour, over 60 of them electrically hauled. Our M.P. for Maldon, Brian Harrison, brought Deedes the M.P. for Ashford, Kent, accustomed to the hurly-burly and brou-ha-ha of the Southern termini along to see it. Harold Few described for half an hour the philosophy of commuter services and the structure of the timetable. Then we went out on to the bridge which overlooks the East side. You can always tell when, as usual, Liverpool Street are in good form. They are strolling through their job. Steady streams are walking, not bustling or shoving, across the concourse. They are giving the ticket collectors time to do their work. They form up on the platforms in little blocks four abreast. Their train slides in, stops on a sixpence, opens its doors precisely in front of them. The blocks take two paces forward into the train. The motorman and guard exchange ends and a brief word on their way. A light goes green. The doors close. A bell rings twice. And another 1,200 are on their way—24,000 an hour on one track. We took Deedes for a ride in the cab. He was pretty complimentary about it all a little while later in the House.

The only discordant note came from Southend. They too enjoyed electrification from both Liverpool Street and Fenchurch Street; about 20 trains an hour, 40 miles odd in generally less than the hour, performing on punctuality, which on the L.T.&S. line was more often than not 100 per cent to time. However, in the bad days of steam traction before the war they had formed an active Travellers' Association. Instead of letting it die of inanition after electrification a few railway enthusiasts kept it going. They were terribly gravelled for lack of matter and started a vendetta against the Divisional Manager at Liverpool Street. He, having established that four trains an hour off peak was too many, reduced them to three, but the one which he took off was the express. 'Even Hitler' thundered the *Southend Standard,* 'did not succeed in doing what Mr. Suddaby has done'. Allegations of spite and vindictiveness began to land up on my table. And indeed in a while Alan had second thoughts and restored the express, though without restoring the previous frequency. Nevertheless, the campaign against him continued. Eventually I lost patience when they wired at Christmas 'Request personal intervention on holiday services ...' I wired back 'Policy of non-intervention at seasons of good will essential. Happy travelling'. This brought a move direct to the Chairman of the B.R.B. and a two page letter about vindictiveness to me. It was easy to reply 'Thou hast appealed unto Caesar. I have withdrawn the light of my countenance from you'. In pulling the Association's collective leg it was a great comfort to have as Mayor of Southend, Owen (Bert) Davis, with whom I had played cricket 30 years ago at Whitemoor among the cow pats. He was with Town Clerk Glen as solid as a rock.

Royal occasions have been familiar for a long time. My first one was unfortunate, namely when I told No. 2 Controller at Cambridge to shunt the empty Royal Train for a string of fast goods and found later that it contained Sir Michael Barrington-Ward. In after years I travelled in charge of Royal trains many times, never without some professional apprehensions which were seldom justified. Good journeys by rail have no history. It is the exceptions which are memorable. Once I arrived at King's Cross to take the Queen to Stockton and found the place bustling, always a bad sign. The front vehicle of the train was a new one, a van with a diesel generator, built by the London Midland. Our engine was an A.4 fitted with a buckeye.

'The buckeyes don't match', said Cyril Palmer. 'There's a difference of two inches in height'.

'Well, part them and use the emergency coupling'.

'We've tried, we can't part them', said Cyril, as nearly miserable as ever I heard him.

We went forward. We pulled and we pushed. We coaxed and we eased. We sloshed it with hammers. We tried to tear them apart. Eventually we had some 20 examiners, fitters, drivers, firemen, guards, inspectors, carriage and wagon foremen, carriage and wagon superintendents, loco. superintendents, traffic managers and a Line Traffic Manager, me. Everyone gave advice. Everyone got hot and bothered and very dirty. At seven minutes before departure we re-attached the rear engine, screwed on all brakes and let the A.4 have a last go. I think the driver with 40 per cent cut off must have slammed the regulator straight to full open. There was an explosion of exhaust and a scream of wheels and motion such as maybe no-one has ever heard. Nevertheless, before she slipped, she must have had an inch or two to grip. The buckeyes parted. I scrubbed off myself what I could with a sponge cloth and took care to be so far from Her Majesty that I could bow only and not shake hands.

The first occasion of 1966 at Liverpool Street also had its moments. The first was when someone told me that the arm had fallen off the Up starter at Tottenham. Arms falling off signals are, let it be said, unusual happenings. The chances against it happening immediately in front of a Royal train are incalculable. Nevertheless it had happened. The proper drill is to station a hand-signalman and to caution all drivers. I was surprised, therefore, when the train eased in smoothly to time. At least I was surprised until I learned later of the enterprise, if not the devotion to rules, of the Great Eastern, which sent a porter with the signal arm clutched to him scampering up the post there to hold it proudly in the 'off' position, while his Sovereign went by under clear signals.

The second moment was when Station-master Harry Onyon having received The Queen at the door of the Royal saloon, turned and said in due form 'May I present my General Manager'. 'My General Manager' took two steps forward and fell over one of the corgis, nearly flat on his face. Luckily the T.V. cameras missed the incident and a moment later when they were on me I was erect. Jean said later when she saw the evening T.V. News, 'You look a bit unfriendly'. 'Not unfriendly, merely repressing a gasp', said I.

I reminded The Queen of this incident last Christmas when they went to Sandringham. Then the corgis were on leads, held in her own left hand. Prince Edward, aged 3, was walking through the booking hall between us, very upright, very clean, very solemn, with a ball clutched in his right hand. I reached down to take his left. He looked up, grinned, transferred the ball from his right to his left, shook hands with his right, transferred the ball from his left to his right, took my right hand with his left and proceeded with me sedately across the red carpet to the train.

Generally we put up a faultless show on Royal occasions. It is one of the things which railwaymen enjoy doing really well. They take enormous pride in taking care of the Royal family. Our inspectors, drivers, guards, superintendents, carriage foremen, timing clerks, commercial contacts with the Palace and all those who are directly associated with the trains. It is remarkable to what lengths railwaymen will go in advertising adverse weather forecasts when there is a choice whether 'They' will return from an engagement by air or by train.

FASTER ALL ALONG THE LINE
BY BRITISH RAILWAYS

# 10

## MERGER OF EASTERN AND NORTH-EASTERN REGIONS

It has been as you see extremely easy to write largely about affairs on the Great Eastern and it would be easy to go on doing so to the exclusion of the coalfields, the steel industry and the oil refineries in the north.

It was one of the strongest arguments in favour of merging the Eastern and North Eastern Regions that within 80 miles of a Headquarters at York there lay the coal of the East Midlands, South Yorkshire, the West Riding, Durham and Northumberland; there lay the steel of Staveley, Sheffield, Scunthorpe, Tees-side and Tyneside; the ports of Grimsby, Immingham, Hull, Tees, Wear and Tyne; oil, wool, chemicals, plastics, light industry, they were all within a couple of hours' ride from York. The Manager would attend to them better if he were there.

I found when I got to Liverpool Street that the two Regions had done a feasibility study of a merger. From this Arthur Dean, then General Manager of the North Eastern Region, and I, drew some evidence and wrote a letter to the Chairman early in January to the effect that the merger was possible, it would have many administrative advantages and it would produce a large saving in managerial costs.

It was difficult for all of us in our welter of coping with the current problems to realise that we had over the years made railways much simpler to manage. We had far fewer things and far fewer people to manage. These are the vital statistics of the combined Eastern and North Eastern Regions in 1966 compared with 1955:—

|  | 1966 | 1955 |
|---|---|---|
| Route miles | 3,600 | 5,100 |
| Terminals | 886 | 2,801 |
| Locomotives | 2,000 | 4,900 |
| Carriages | 5,800 | 10,500 |
| Road Vehicles | 2,400 | 3,900 |
| Marshalling Yards | 64 | 226 |
| Train miles — passenger | 52m. | 51m. |
| Train miles — freight | 30m. | 40m. |
| Staff | 81,900 | 150,000 |
| Revenue | £135m | £131m |

More revenue, less equipment and staff could add up to fewer managers.

We had then two choices, either to cut the Headquarters at York and at Liverpool Street down to size, each in its own place; or to combine the two at York. The arguments against the choice which we adopted were that here again was another re-organisation of which we all had had our bellyful over the last ten years, and that any reorganisation was a distraction from the main direction of effort, namely our statutory duty to provide railway services with due regard to safety, efficiency and economy and to break even taking one year with another. Secondly it would mean a major upheaval for the staff at Liverpool Street, a thing which would be anti-social in the extreme. Thirdly that the new combined Region would be as large and therefore as unmanageable as that Behemoth, the London Midland.

In favour of the choice we calculated firstly that the administrative savings would be of the order of £1.6m. a year; secondly that we should not reap the 'economics of scale' unless we combined; thirdly that if we combined, to do so at York was the self evident choice, because 80 per cent of our freight business originated within 80 miles of York, as did 70 per cent of our inter-city passengers; fourthly to move offices out of London was in line with the Government's declared policy; fifthly the movement of coal amounting to tens of millions of tons to the new power stations across the regional boundary would be better managed in one hand. This argument also reversed of course, the recent changes in boundary which had separated Leeds and Bradford from King's Cross.

In commenting on the arguments against the merger we accepted the argument in principle about reorganisations, 'when you reorganise, you bleed'. I quoted from someone who lectures to our Staff College at Woking. We recognised the social problems and would minimise them. We doubted whether Bill Johnson and the Euston Confederacy would agree that the London Midland was unmanageable. If so, why had they only a few years ago enlarged it by annexing Banbury, Birmingham, Birkenhead, and much of Wales? Why were some of them now talking of mounting a *drang nach osten* with Sheffield as its primary objective? In any event, although the revenue of the new Region would be £15m. or so a year larger than that of the London Midland, the physical equipment would be one third less and the staff one fifth less. In another comparison, whereas the new Region would have under 82,000 staff, the Western Region a few years ago had 92,000. No-one ever argued that Sir James Milne or Keith Grand could not manage a railway of that size.

The arguments added up in favour of the merger with Headquarters at York. Maybe I was the principal doubter. I hated reorganisations because they were distractions. I was profoundly bored by administration processes. My fun in life was managing a bit of railway. Indeed reorganisation has been the only subject in this book which has brought out of me the word 'bored'. And I liked bits of railway to manage where I could get around to get to know people and to be known. I distrusted myself in something the size of the London Midland. On a free vote in the House I would have been a 'Noe'. But it wasn't a free vote of the House; it was a press gang job. I set out to do it with my strength and to get it out of my hair as quickly as I could.

It became fairly quickly evident that among the top echelon I was alone in doing it with my strength. On December 23rd I had written to the Chairman 'given good support and reasonable speed of decision in matters which are not within our authority I expect to complete the task of setting up the new Region early in 1967'. On January 5th Arthur Dean and I met the Chairman and agreed readily on the principles. On the same day the Chairman wrote to the Minister seeking agreement to reducing the number of Regional Railway Boards to five. He had to do this because the Transport Act 1962 had legislated flatfooted 'In the first instance there shall be six Regional Railway Boards ... but the Minister may after consulting the Railway Board by order alter the number of Regional Railway Boards'.

'O Mount Vesuvius' cried Tessa in the Gondoliers 'here we are in arithmetic' and so we were for 12 months. On January 6th the

Chairman wrote to me 'You can do nothing further until I get clearance from the Minister'. Nevertheless we drew up a timetable:

| | |
|---|---|
| Ministerial Consent. | February. 1966. |
| Public and Trade Union announcement. | February. |
| Assessment of H.Q. staff complete. | February/March. |
| Appointment Management Team. | April. |
| Consultation Sectional Councils. | April/June. |
| Designate appointments effective. | June. |
| Appointments of remaining staff. | July/November. |
| Part new office ready. | January. 1967. |
| Eastern Region H.Q. set up at York. | January. |

We set up a steering Group for a 'study' as it would have to be until the Minister consented to make her order. The group was three people only; J. E. H. Skerrett, Assistant General Manager (Staff) at York, F. E. Longhorn, Establishment Officer at Liverpool Street, and J. Johnson, Secretary of the Eastern Railways Board.

For a month we seemed to be on time. On February 8th the Chairman replying to a letter from the Minister wrote to her 'Now that I have your agreement in principle we will let the Unions know what is proposed and start discussing the objectives in detail with them'. I commented 'How soon can we come out into the open?' On February 17th, A.G.M. (Staff) Pearson Armstrong met Jagger at the Board and reached understanding on the broad pattern of the structure of organisation, and more important, that the levels of salary would be those applicable to the London Midland. Many people selected would therefore enter the new Region on promotion. The group went bashing ahead. They reported on February 10th that the principles and the timetable were feasible. On February 24th Alex Dunbar, Arthur Dean and I met Laurie Orchard of the British Transport Officers' Guild and

John Bothwell of the Transport Salaried Staff Association for the first meeting in consultation.

However, on February 24th I find that I appealed to the Chairman 'to clear the log jam before Parliament adjourns'. He replied verbally 'you cannot expect a decision with a General Election pending', and followed this up on February 28th 'The Minister will go no further until we have given more information about the effects of the amalgamation on the staff'. I replied 'Bad news; it will put us two months at least behind our Target Date, lengthen the period of uncertainty for the staff, and lengthen the period of rundown whereby increasingly either people will be working harder or the march of progress will be slower ... the business of the country must go on. It does not seem that the Minister has an alibi on the score of the Election'. Whether she had or hadn't, we got no decision. Of course I should have known. I have had previous experience. When I was up at Oxford, urging Blackie Frankel with every circumstance of logic why we should continue on a footpath across a corner of a field in which there was a distant bull. I was defeated entirely by 'I won't say yes and I won't say no and I won't get over that stile'.

The nation returned a Socialist Government with a handsome majority. But it did not increase the pace of the merger. It did the reverse. The Chairman told me in April 'There are more important things to think about', namely the reorganisations which are evolving into the 'Sundries Division', the Conurbation Authorities, the 'A and B railway', the manoeuvres with the deficit all foreshadowed in the White Paper on Transport published just before the Election. Dunbar, who had cleared in March with Dean and me the principal structure of the organisation and names for the chief appointments and had agreed to put them to the other members before the end of April, did not produce the results for six months.

I do not propose to go on with the story. You, like me, are bored with it. It is enough to say that in December the Minister suddenly made an order. George, Lord Lindgren entered a prayer in the House of Lords against it, which after debate he withdrew. We got an instruction to set up the Eastern Region's Headquarters at York on January 1st. It gave us 11 days notice, of which by reason of Christmas and New Year seven were dies non. Ha Ha. Entering fully into the spirit of the whole enterprise six of us actually got there. Pearson Armstrong (Staff), John Brenan (Finance), Charles Whitworth (Admin.), Frank Longhorn (Reorganisation), John Johnson (Board Secretary) and myself. We were joined in top management by North Eastern Derek Barrie (Commercial), Arthur Dytch (Technical) and Scottish, James Urquhart (Movements). It will take longer than the ten months which this book will be in publication, from the time of writing these words, for the principal move. We are a year behind, at a cost maybe of around £2m. for the administrative savings deferred, plus the cost of the distraction from our proper jobs in savings or reserves not realised. The moral is, when you put your hand to the plough, don't drag your feet.

When in March it became abundantly clear that the people at the British Railways Board who ought to have been pushing the Minister into a decision and pushing me into carrying it out with abounding energy, were going to do nothing of the kind, I gave myself more time for doing a bit of railway work, namely to attending to our duty of breaking even. This duty on British Railways has been a very simple one over the last ten years, which is all the time it is since we plunged into deficit. It is a matter of reducing the number of staff on the payroll.

Since 1955 the level of receipts in terms of money has been virtually static. Whatever have been the enquiries, the appraisals, the re-appraisals, however intelligently the marketing managers have manoeuvred, however robustly the B.R.B. have argued about London commuters before the Tribunal, whatever successes we have had with oil and motor cars and cement and so on, we get no more money into the till. See the graph on page 109.

In real terms of course the revenue has gone down. Since wages account for two-thirds of our expenses, we can only therefore pay the same wages, let alone higher wages, by reducing the number of staff, or by allowing an increase in the deficit, which by law we cannot have at all. So the unfortunate staff must themselves pay for their own improved conditions of service by making their fellows redundant. In this they have had some success. The numbers have declined since 1957, from 574,000 to 353,000, while the deficit in terms of the operating ratio has risen from 105 to 117 (1965).

Within these figures it is interesting to note the good performers; the Southern have improved from 108 to 96, the Western from 123 via a high point of 138 in 1961 to 108; and the Eastern from 102 via 106 in 1961 to 90. The North Eastern although worse overall—88 to 94—went via a high point in 1962 of 112. They share with the Eastern the distinction not only of being East Coast but of being a part of British Railways which can claim to carry out their statutory duty of breaking even.

By February 1966 the Eastern Region's part in this achievement began to wobble. Receipts were hesitating. Iron and steel, general merchandise, parcels and sundries, were feeling the effects of the impending recession. Expenditure was rising, especially in the Sheffield and Liverpool Street Divisions. The budget results were looking horrible. In the event it needed little management to set the thing again on its proper course. The Management of the Region at Headquarters had become inhibited by disciplines beyond all reason. When in 1965 Roy Hammond sent me a few sets of the minutes of the weekly Management Conference so that

I could pick up the threads I was struck at once by the number of minutes which began 'The B.R.B. have laid it down' or 'It is the B.R.B.'s wish' or, worse, 'It is not the B.R.B.'s wish'. To one who enjoyed and indeed fostered the spirit of free enterprise at Paddington—as had Raymond before me—this wording was a clear pointer to trouble.

We began by expunging the letters 'B.R.B.' from our minutes. We set free the highly competent and highly rewarded managers at Headquarters and in the Divisions to do their proper and highly rewarding jobs. For good measure we added to the attack on costs one of the Assistants (Special Duties), who I discovered very reluctantly and very slowly working out in a back room how to reduce the G.N. main fine from four to two tracks. Since he was the best rough-and-tumble operating one man razor gang that I know, old John Dedman joined the spearhead and became ten years younger overnight.

Within two months our budget began to go right. By the end of 1966 we had missed our target of revenue by some £0.3m. but had reduced our expenditure below budget by £1.6m. Compared with 1965 revenue was up by £2.3m.; expenditure was down by £2.0m.; our operating ratio was 90. This, my masters, is what management of railways is all about, if you would only take heed. Set people simple, understandable duties. Tell them to work their bit of railway safely, efficiently, profitably. Then set them free to get on with the job.

This philosophy did not find ready acceptance at the British Railways Board, and we were at odds accordingly. I resisted interference with my business and grumped that they were not doing their proper jobs. Among the subjects reserved to the Centre, many were not going well. In design diesel locomotives, electric locomotives, electric multiple units, wagons for liner trains, cranes for liner trains, were all in trouble, some of it deep trouble. The Workshops authority was badly behind schedule in overhauls and badly over its target for costs. The staff boys had so far failed to secure an agreement on the Open Terminal for liner trains, or to enforce the year old agreement on single manning of locomotives; or to produce the promised scheme for incentives on short distance freight trains. The commercial and operating people had produced no new major ideas since Liner trains, Merry-go-round, and the oil agreement of about five years before.

In spite therefore of the references to the deficit, what we were doing—in the order in which the Chairman mentioned them at one meeting—was the Sundries Division, the National Freight Organisation, the Eastern/North Eastern Merger, the deficit, the Conurbation Transport Authorities. Three of these, Sundries, and N.F.O., and Conurbations, were a fragmentation of British Railways. The new philosophy seemed to be that the railways should be 'professional'. They should consist of engineers who constructed and maintained in the latest term an infra-structure and of operators who ran trains. All else was to be done by someone else. I am a believer in getting the incentives in the right place. Under these proposals who would have the incentive to put traffic on the railways. As the Chairman said, the first action of the Sundries Division must be to get powers to take traffic throughout by road.

I was therefore very much out of sympathy with the way the Board were running the business and had, before coining to York, indicated to the Chairman that I did not want to stay in the service longer than was necessary to set the merger well in hand.

# 11

## THE WAY OUT

On my 60th birthday the family—except Bron—changed their attitude; and not subtly either. Instead of 'many happy returns' it was 'happy birthday'. Once—off. Bron's 'many happy returns' was accompanied by a rough hug which conveyed that she was thinking 'any moment now'. Nevertheless, here I am, still lingering on months later. Jean is doing some subliminal advertising for retirement, but I am not finding the moment of truth easily.

I do not imagine any railwayman knows how deeply he is involved. I thumbed a lift from a lorry a few months ago. When the driver heard I was a railwayman he said 'my dad was a driver at Neath Depot. Retired three years ago you know. It is a job to get my wife in his house. Talks railways from morning till night'.

Talking isn't enough. I have talked railways interminably, and seldom sense: but the Old Man's rough and tumble managers are doers: and in retirement, there is no doing. Will writing satisfy the need? 'Music' wrote Wordsworth 'is emotion recollected in tranquillity'. It might work. John Sharp Grant, who cured my heart trouble ten years ago by telling me it didn't exist, says I must get a job. Easy for an Engineer or an Accountant; indeed hard to avoid: Gliffie Gold so it is said, when he wanted to take his ease after retirement, solved that one by writing himself in at the Labour Exchange as Railway Mechanical Engineer (Steam). For me, who would employ a General Manager who when asked his supplementary question would reply 'bumped-up timetable clerk?' At least not at the end of the Aldeburgh branch, defunct.

Nevertheless the odds in favour are pretty formidable. Jean; Jeremy in Stockholm; Joslin in Bechuanaland; Michael and Rosalie at Harvard. We would like a trip round them while it would be an active pleasure. I want to get down to 14 at golf; fish for a month a year. I want, badly, to write another book.

I do *not* want—for five years is too short—to get involved in the 125 m.p.h. or, more rightly, the 250 m.p.h. railway: or in Hovercraft: I am not really interested in the Container Age. I am thoroughly bored by reorganisations—the National Freight Authority, the amalgamation of the Eastern and North Eastern Regions and of the Humberside Divisions. I resent—o mea culpa—being lectured by the British Railways Board, severally and collectively. They bring out the worst in me, which is rotten for them and no fun for me. Beyond everything it is that democracy has wrapped management up in a parcel of Consultation. I am no longer 'the Guv'nor' to be argued with and obeyed, but the Chairman of the Management side of the Consultation Procedure to be resisted, circumvented, delayed—may be one day walked-out-on. The pace is slow, slow, slow.

I see I have just blamed democracy rather than myself for the pace being slow. Then indeed I am lingering on. As I told you, decisions are not made; they emerge.

1ST

THE STATION

# POSTSCRIPT

Soon after the initial publication of this book, Thomas T. Tabor of Madison, New Jersey, a formidable hammer of railway management on both sides of the Atlantic, wrote out of long friendship that the book had no ending. And of course it hadn't. The preceding chapter as written shewed me waffling about retiring but having no date or occasion in mind.

In the end to find the moment of truth for retirement was easy. I did not have a choice. Or rather I did, but the other side of it was only what Bob Hilton, on an earlier occasion, called with some difficulty 'instant dismissal'.

Looking back, it is clear enough now to me that to have retired on the crest of the wave of goodwill and success at Paddington would have been right. But like the girl who can't say no I had always done what I was asked to do on the railway, even when it was put as grumpily as: 'You seem to get people to work for you—I can't think why—so it had better be you for the merger'.

And of course 1967 was the wrong year for anyone to be around who thought railways could be a success and who tried accordingly. However often in detail I disagreed with the Great and Good Doctor's approach—'Get rid of what you can't support. Expand what you can'—he was heading for success. In 1966 and 1967 the recipe had changed. In anticipation of the 1968 Transport Bill the accountants were at work to justify the greatest possible subsidy and the greatest possible write-off of capital by the Government. It was therefore logical to take the gloomiest view of prospects and to calculate that the largest number of activities lost money by the greatest possible margin. Failure was a positive advantage. The larger the deficit the greater the success. It was brilliantly done. In the outcome around £140m a year was lifted from B.R. and left with the taxpayer. My share of that in tax is around £8 a week.

I went to York and found tolerance combined with doubt. Luckily Deputy General Manager Derek Barrie was there. At our first meeting of the top management he tentatively cracked a small, nutty jest and promptly looked down over his spectacles at the bowl of his pipe to await reactions. They were at least favourable enough for him to take over the job of keeping us as cheerful as could be expected.

We began with a message in the Management Bulletin for January 1967:—

'AMALGAMATION OF EASTERN AND NORTH EASTERN REGIONS.

Let us put first things first.

First, then, our duty as railwaymen; it is to "provide railway services having due regard for safety, efficiency and economy" and to "break even financially, taking one year with another". This is the law. Let us test our decisions and actions by whether they keep faith with the letter and with the spirit of the law. First and last, our duty as railwaymen.

It is in line with that duty that the Eastern and North Eastern Regions combine, and integrate the railways from Berwick to

King's Cross, from Harwich to Bradford. There is one boundary the less, one less river to cross, one less barrier on the way to fulfilment of our duty.

Remember that already the East Coast Regions stand at the head of British Railways in safety, efficiency and economy. On one assessment they "break even". These things have not just happened. People have done it, much the same people who will carry the new region from strength to strength. G. F. FIENNES.'

The task of merging the staff of the two headquarters, Eastern and North Eastern, was in the hands of Pearson Armstrong and Frank Longhorn. It was good luck—or good management because Willie Thorpe was trying to induce Pearson to go to Euston— that they were there. They succeeded in bringing around 700 willing or reluctant people and their families from London and in sweetening the pill for most of them by promotion. My part in all this consisted, firstly, in a public row with the builders of York for putting up the prices of houses in our face, which may have moderated the pace a little; and secondly, in the most successful piece of public relations I have ever managed. One day we had the Archbishop to lunch. He asked how we were getting on and then whether he could help. I jumped at the offer. The upshot was that when we had a party from London showing them York, Dr. and Mrs. Coggan came to the tea. They played a big part in the welcome which York gave our people. Few of those who made the move regretted the change.

Whether now they regret it is less certain after the adoption of the McKinsey report that Regional Headquarters should be abolished and that York should be broken up into Territories. There were rumours that such might be the intention almost as soon as we got to York; and in the spring of 1967 we sought and received an assurance to the contrary. Nevertheless, in Dr. M. R. Bonavia's book *The Organisation of British Railways* he writes:

'Certain Board Members felt that a more centralised and functionally directed organisation would be an improvement. These views took shape in a draft memorandum, sponsored by the Vice-Chairman, Mr. P. H. Shirley, and the Financial Member, Mr. P. G. James, dated 6th April, 1967. The memorandum made the following points ... Organisationally, responsibility for main workshops had been taken away from the Regions; standardisation had replaced Regional preferences over a wide front; engineering practices and purchase of equipment and supplies, and design and development, had all been centralised. The Board were moving towards the position where rolling stock was owned and allocated by Headquarters. Banking and computer services were already centralised; management development and training were centrally overseen and controlled; planning of new investment projects, technical development and research were also central. Commercial planning and market development were directed from the Centre, particularly in regard to advertising. So was product development, such as the Freightliner, Motorail and Inter-City train services. Major customers such as the oil companies, and the N.C.B., and similarly nationally operating customers were dealt with by Headquarters. The formation of a Sundries Division including the road collection and delivery fleet as a centrally controlled organisation had brought under a single authority one of the major, traditionally local, railway operations ...'

The concrete proposal embodied in the paper was that the Board should have seven full-time functional members in addition to the Chairman and Vice-Chairman. These functional members 'should have authority and should be required to exercise it.'... Each functional member would cover a number of departments. Heads of departments would be responsible to their functional members; under them there would be some sixteen to twenty operating Divisions ranging from five for the London and South East area to only one in Scotland.... 'The Divisional Manager must not countermand or seek to apply his own preference or interpretation on any matter without reference to headquarters and must accept any confirmed decision as binding.'... 'Replacing the regions, there would be an intermediate level of authority in the shape of Area Managers, who would be primarily regarded as members of the Headquarters staff. In the area office there would be a small secretarial staff but not a functional staff. The Area Managers were intended to be the local projection of the Board and to have a status intermediate between that of Member and Chief Officer. This would not, however, confer power to override Chief Officers' decisions. They would be essentially advisory on Board issues and have no responsibility for divisional performance and no concern with the running of the railway ...'

This memorandum was discussed between the Chairman, the Vice-Chairman and Mr. H. C. Johnson, General Manager of the London Midland Region, for the General Managers.

But no one told the chap who was briskly marching in the opposite direction with his troops around York.

However, after discussions a more cautious paper was produced and circulated in draft form to the Board Members. This formed basis of the Board's proposals to the Joint Steering Group dated 26th April, 1967. It proposed that the present system of Regional Managers should continue for at least several years.

We took a flat, Jean and I, overlooking the racecourse and next to the house owned by a great predecessor, Jenkin-Jones. J. J., like Sir Michael Barrington-Ward when he retired, had padlocked his lips about railways and had turned to other things—B.-W. to directing a mining engineering company, J. J. to governing hospitals. At 80, spare and alert, he put me to shame, fat, bald and ugly at 61. So I started to sweat it out of myself.

The Institute at York, built little by little by Engineer John Miller, had as a by-blow of some project such as a four-tracking three squash courts. After a tentative trial by myself I started to organise an old man's gang. There were two volunteers, the public relations officer, Brigadier Stuart Knox, and the marketing manager, Eric Jones. Neither was old within the terms of reference; both ran like rabbits. Eric had been a heavy-weight for Belsize. To hear him get under way from the rear of the court behind me and thunder towards a lob was a daunting experience. God knows how a ring ever held him. Perhaps it didn't because he braked with difficulty. He ended this phase of his career by running full tilt into a wall with the point of his shoulder and chipping the bone. Soon afterwards, running round Stuart Knox, I tore a vein in my leg—and serve me right.

Jean and I took to tennis, indoors in the Institute and outside on the hard courts at Leeman Road; and that too came to a sudden end. We were playing a singles and by dint of running like a rabbit for the wide ones Jean was leading 5–2 when she sank in a heap beyond the backhand doubles line—left leg forward, right arm backward, arms and neck and head in a graceful line, like Pavlova's dying swan. I laughed. She looked at me coldly.

'I have fallen on my wrist' she said.

'Luckily I am an Officer Brother of the Order of St. John,' I replied and went into a patter of deformity and irregularily, flexing her fingers and asking whether it hurt, which it did.

'Not broken,' I judged, 'We will treat you for shock'.

And I led the way to the bar.

However, three days later Dr. Fraser McKenzie sent her for an X-ray. A hairline fracture it was.

Somewhere along the line—about the end of January 1967 I think—I had finished the preceding chapters of this book. The title was the *The Fat Controller*. Mr. Awdry cordially assented to my own view that the operating methods on the railways which I tried to run were essentially those which he described in *James, The Red Engine* and in many others—that is to say, the manager gets the job round his neck and is rescued by his engines and men because they have fun in their work. However, the publishers, who were a very market-conscious lot of young men, thought 'The Fat Controller' would distort the image and themselves suggested *I Tried to Run a Railway*. So *I Tried* ... it became. And over the horizon peeped a small cloud no greater than a man's hand.

Sometimes I have wondered whether any event which I attended or which I initiated would go down in history. In a hundred years' time which events of the period 1930–1970 will earn a chapter, a page or a paragraph in a railway history? The part of the railways in the war? Nationalisation and the days of the Hurcumcision? The Beeching era? Freightliner? Merry-go-Round? Inter-City? At a distance all these things diminish.

The one incontrovertible 'first' I did encounter was the action of a signalman at Conington in deliberately derailing an express train at speed. 'First' and, we trust, 'only'.

It was in March 1967 and at a week-end. I was at Aldeburgh. When the phone rings at dead of night a General Manager apprehends trouble: an accident to a passenger train with people killed. Usually he gets up and goes with all deliberate speed, because others will have got on with the work of rescue, of reforming the service and of clearing the line. These others, train crews, first-aid squads, district inspectors, controllers, divisional managers, do not take to General Managers who come too soon, asking "Have you thought of so-and-so?" or urging "Do it this way". You must never take the fun out of other people's work. So

I dug out Jean's car which happened to be nearest in the garage. This was a black Morris 1000 convertible dating from 1964. Just before Christmas that year, having some money in the bank, as for some reason and for the first and only time we always had when we were at Paddington, I said to her:

'Would you like a car for Christmas?'

'I have always wanted'—this like a flash—'a Morris 1000 convertible, black.'

So I went to the local garage.

'Well,' said Russ, 'the Morris 1000 will go out of production this year and you will lose money. A convertible is highly unpractical in this climate. And they don't make them black.'

This seemed to be game, set and match to Russ, but Jean just repeated it.

"I have always wanted ..."

She got it. They put a white one back in the furnace and blacked it. A lovely little car.

I set off across East Anglia through the clear, still night very much at peace. There were no longer any tensions about going to an accident. The violence of the wreck itself is over in probably half a minute. The rescue is unlikely to have taken more than half-an-hour. After three hours the scene will be one of arc-lights, of cranes, of wisps of drifting steam and of the disciplined restoration of order.

I began to compose a limerick about a curate of the last village. 'Why', said the people of Coddenham, 'Do you preach in your pants? you look odd in 'em.' But he wouldn't take them off, asserting 'he'd face Bishop or Vicar or God in 'em.' Which brought me to Bury St. Edmunds, a host of flashing torches and a police sergeant who with the utmost courtesy said:

'Would you mind telling me, sir, who you are and where you are going?'

'I am a railway General Manager. I am going to an accident.'

As I said it the story on both counts seemed a bit thin, but he lost not a whit of his manners.

'Would you mind getting out, sir?'

And he called up a posse which searched the car from stem to stern. Then he looked at me, but I wasn't having that. I stalked to the car and drove away with a look which dared him to stop me. About an hour later I stopped on the top of Alconbury Hill, climbed a little knoll and looked round to locate the arc-lights on the jibs of the breakdown cranes. Ten minutes later I drove up to Conington South.

It was a proper mess. The 22.30 sleeper from King's Cross had (until we established the cause) 'become derailed.' The train had broken in half. The front half was out of sight to the northward and the rear four coaches had dug into the track, destroying it completely and in the process littering the scene with torn-off bogies, brake blocks, brake rods, fan belts, bits of dynamo and glass. One bogie lay right-side up athwart the track, 50 yards ahead of the wreck.

The New England crane was re-railing the two derailed coaches in the front half. The King's Cross crane had started on the rear. Richard Hardy (Divisional Manager), Edwin Howell (Movements Manager) and Colin Morris (Motive Power Superintendent) had all the processes proceeding.

As yet they hadn't a clue what had caused it. There had been no other train about. The track was part of the best race-track on the East Coast, which meant the best in the country. The train was a crack express, examined before it left the carriage sidings and again at King's Cross. Nevertheless, no railwayman can contemplate that a good train on good track at normal speed can 'become derailed'. Behind every accident there is some person or persons—designer, maintainer or operator—who has by a sin of omission or commission caused it. The evidence, if we could find it, would be somewhere around or in the wreck.

The first thing we came up with was that on the last vehicle of the front portion the massive head of the rear buckeye coupler was fractured. Cause of the accident? Or effect of it? The missing piece could well have derailed the train. If we found it in the wreck with a wheel mark on it, that piece would be the cause. Metallurgical examination would probably lead to the culprit.

The second thing we found was that the tip of the switch blade on the points leading from the main line to the goods line was slightly burred over; and that between the blade and the stock rail was the bruise of a wheel or wheels. It looked as if the points had been open when the train passed. But, as we argued through the night, this solution became more and more impossible; and if 'impossible' is in itself a superlative, then for something to be more impossible shews how egg-bound our minds became. For the points were locked by a lock-bar, an electrical track circuit and by the home signal at clear. No damage was apparent to the locking or to the stretcher bar at the nose of the points. If a wheel had forced its way between the blade and the stock rail some distortions would have been obvious.

The dawn came across the fen, slow, misty and infinitely chill. And with the light came the recovery of the missing part of the buck-eye head, lying clear, well ahead of the point of derailment. It was an effect of the accident, not the cause.

We went into the Tool Van for mugs of tea and doorstep sandwiches. We came out warmer but still unenlightened. By now the work of clearance was almost done. The torn-off bogies were neatly ranked by the up line, the coach bodies beyond the signalbox, the mangled rails and sleepers were pushed aside and a calf-dozer was burrowing out the old ballast to prepare for new track. At that moment Richard was handed a telegram. A very slow smile spread across his face. Coming from the Research Department at Derby, it read: 'Touch nothing till I come'.

To be fair, they had a problem. The derailments of freight vehicles on plain track were continuing and spreading to unexpected modern types—oil tanks, bulk cement wagons and so on. They needed to take a hard look at a derailed express. And in the event their report about the track and the train was a most powerful re-inforcement of our own conclusions that whatever had happened at Conington should not stop us running expresses at 100 miles an hour and sleeping quietly in our beds.

At around 9.30 Richard and I parted, I to visit the hospital in Peterborough to ask after the casualties and to go on to York. I wrote to Richard wishing him luck with the enquiry. I added that if I was Dorothy Sayers writing a thriller it would be the signalman who had done it and he would have done it like this...

So taken was I with my theory that I began a novel around a theme, full of railways and sex, than which there are no more absorbing subjects. It will never see the light of day now because, before it was finished, the signalman at Conington, who had left the railway not long after the accident, was arrested, tried and gaoled for having derailed the train, using the principles which I had set out.

We had another accident to an express in 1967 which took the taste of Conington out of my mouth. I knew that at Conington some railwaymen had done something scaly quite outside the forgivable endearing things which railwaymen do. At Thirsk the two enginemen behaved in a way which warmed the cockles of my heart. They were crossing the Vale of York with the 12 noon out of King's Cross, well into their swing at around 80 m.p.h. With no warning about 400 yards ahead of them a cloud of dust billowed across slow and main lines. Within a moment a derailed wagon lurched out of it into their path. Driver John

Evans threw out all the anchors—vacuum brake, Westinghouse brake, foot off the dead man's pedal. He even thought of using his sands. Second man Dennis Smith reached down for his bag, took out three detonators, opened the offside door of the cab and braced himself against the post. If he survived, he could stop the trains on the up line from running into the wreck to come. At the last moment before impact Evans threw himself to his right. Still doing around 40 m.p.h., the engine tore into 100 tons of derailed steel and cement. It ripped out the lefthand side of the locomotive and of the first six coaches. Seven passengers died, but not Evans or Smith.

They went off to carry out their duty in protecting their train. About an hour later I saw them on the scene. When we had done talking I sent them off homewards towards Gateshead in my car. Chauffeur Ron told me afterwards that within a few miles his brakes had failed.

'God', they cried, 'This is bloody unsafe. Take us to the nearest station'.

The events in this story make up one of the many reasons why railways must above all else cherish the Men of the Front End. They must select, train, discipline and turn them into Evanses and Smiths. It is the Front End only which positively gets us there safely, speedily, punctually, comfortably. All others stand aside or actively prevent us getting there. Paddington, so I am told, still remembers a Bank Holiday in 1964 when, with trains standing back nearly as far as Ealing I went into one of the boxes.

'What is this box?' I asked.

'The Paddington Arrival Box.'

'The Paddington Arrival Prevention Box', I amended.

In the meantime, at the beginning of 1967, it was fun to see how well we were doing. The Inter-City service, both on the East Coast Route and in East Anglia, was attracting more people and earning more money—a lot more money; so much so that on the East Coast its surplus paid for the whole of the track and signalling without any contribution from freight. The commuters were quiet, which is as high a compliment to local managers as commuters can pay. Rural trains were holding their own.

On the freight side at long last the National Coal Board were beginning to equip collieries for Merry-go-Round. The large power stations at Thorpe Marsh, High Marnham, Cottam, Ferrybridge and the rest were built or building and would push the tonnage by Merry-go-Round up to over 30 million a year within ten years of the idea being born. In Freightliner the technical trials were well ahead and all seemed set fair for a similar tonnage in a similar time. The coal port at Immingham for 3 million tons a year had received authority. Steel was doing well. Company trains of oil, cement, sand, barley, motor cars were much in evidence. Going around I could see more of the 'emerging' railway than of George Stephenson's. Beeching opened a lot more things, including minds to ideas, than he closed. And, of course, in 1966 the Eastern Region southern end had made a surplus of over £3m which more than compensated for the deficit on the North Eastern.

To my competitive mind maybe the nub of the matter was how much better, demonstrably better, we were than the Euston Confederacy. We were earning each of us around £140 million that year in our budget. The Eastern Region was doing it with about a third less stations, marshalling yards, locomotives and carriages, and with about a fifth less staff. And our record of safety was markedly better, this in spite of the two bad accidents to passenger trains.

However, it was not long before 1967 began to go awry financially. Within six months receipts had declined by £5 million and expenses had been cut by only £2 million. Our surplus had vanished. All sorts of people had all sorts of reasons. Government squeezes, mild winters, the steel cycle, the lot. And they may have been right because the other regions were in the same decline. Nevertheless I thought that the people who should have been searching for traffic or cutting costs or both were spending too much time re-organising. I said so, probably more than once, at the B.R.B.'s monthly meeting with its General Managers. I find that I wrote to the Operating Member:

Dear Fred,

Many thanks for yours. I gather my points which I made at the invitation of the Chairman—what I would do to get off the plateau if I were him—have been crudely summarised in 222 as "Sack the Board". Not so; *absit omen:* God forbid.

(1) It is the prime duty of the members and chief officers of the B.R.B. to devise new ideas and systems of transport by rail. No new major idea like Liner trains or Merry-go-Round has emerged in four years. You have very able people capable of ideas. Therefore they are being distracted by other things. Stop distracting them by other things.

(2) Stop distracting regions with re-organisation.

(3) There are wide differences in the performances of regions which are similar in industrial and social structure. Why? Find out and put the General Managers on the spot.

(4) Apply (3) to the Workshops but since you have no comparison with other Workshops, test them by what Sir Steuart Mitchell forecast.

All this is, of course, in the context of the deficit. Contrariwise, the B.R.B. may choose to go on 'managing' and reorganising. Points (1)–(4) are merely what I would do if I were Chairman. I meant them very deeply. Do the B.R.B. really mean it about the deficit? As to (3), John Brenan and I, who have already done some primitive arithmetic, will develop it and send it to you.

After a career of believing that railways should and could stand on their own feet and of trying to run my bit of railway accordingly it was hard to come to terms with the New Higher Thought.

The story of the rest of 1967 has no place in this postscript. We had labour troubles, guards' disputes, loco disputes, terminal disputes, all either begun at national level or taken there to be managed. We had a lot about rural railways in which, with Pay Trains, the Eastern Region made something of a dent in the Beeching figures and moved some way toward the policy that local authorities should contribute to the cost of the service.

I do not propose to tell the story of my departure in detail. I went hurriedly from the scene. It must be enough that on the 22nd September, 1967 I received the following letter:

It has come to the notice of the Board that you have written a book for publication dealing with your period as General Manager of the Western and Eastern Regions.

I write to draw your attention to the instruction of 2nd November, 1964 which calls for such material for publication to be submitted for clearance before publication and to ask you to do this before the book or any part of it is published.

The Board would take an extremely serious view of any publication by you without clearance. Signed: E. Harding.

I replied disarmingly but was summoned on the 25th September, was told that it was intolerable that I should continue to serve the Board and that there could be no argument. I went away, like the elephant's child, a little warm but not at all astonished. At the door was The Press who seemed to have prior knowledge and to treat the whole affair, surprisingly, as a national event. Let it be said that over the next weeks—and it went on for weeks—Press, Radio and T.V. treated me with warm and most friendly consideration.

Among the reviewers, Sir John Elliot wrote: 'There has been nothing like it since just before the 1914 war ... the great thing is to know when to let it (pent-up insubordination) boil over and the answer broadly is never.'

Said Richard Hope: 'The autobiography is a remarkably mild and reasonable document. Personal invective is entirely absent and the man who comes in for the most direct criticism is the author himself.

Well, if you have got so far, you have judged whether John or Richard is right. There was a large and continuing post bag. The one which I liked best was from Passenger Guard Bill Moss. Bill and I used jointly to work his trains on the Loughton line in 1944–45, I telling him how to get his train along the road, he telling me how to run the railway. Bill wrote: 'I saw in the paper this morning of your terrible bad ways—don't bother with them any more'.

But of course I do. Once a railwayman, always a railwayman; a member of the most exclusive club, nationally and internationally, in the world. Bill Williams, who came from Shell in the Beeching era, used to say: 'Gerry, I have never heard so much talk and it is all about railways. What on earth do you find in it?' It is true. Two men in a pub, both railwaymen—and it's railways; even with one railwaymen—railways. No one really knows why. It has something to do with the basic things of life and death, always being about; something to do with the disciplined independence of working a timetable and a rule book with little direct supervision; something to do with the measured repetitive patterns, rather like cricket. Most of all it is to do with the closely knit society and the common language.

It has nothing to do with 'the Divisional Manager must not countermand or seek to apply his own preference or interpretation on any matter without reference to headquarters'. Contrariwise, Divisional Managers, Inspectors, Controllers, Drivers, Guards,

Shunters, Ticket Collectors—the lot—have free-standing, tall-standing jobs. The breath of life to them and to the railway that they serve is their rugged, self-disciplined independence. Those who do not understand have no business on a railway.

As Groucho Marx once said: 'I wouldn't think of joining a club which would elect me as a member'.

# INDEX